YouTube Secrets Hacks for Beginners

A Complete Guide for Making Money with Video Content and Become a YouTube Influencer with Strategic Content and Monetization Techniques

By: **Blake Preston & Brian Scott Fitzgerald**

Published By: **Fitzgerald Publishing Group**

How to Make Money Online: THE SERIES

I created a series of 12 (twelve) books on How to Make Money Online.

Feel free to read any of my books in the series, which can be found on my Author page on Amazon at:

You can visit this link or Scan this QR code to get access

https://www.amazon.com/author/brianscottfitzgerald.

Contents

Your Free Gift

Thank you for your purchase; I'm offering my readers the FREE PDF version of ChatGPT Prompts.

To get almost instant access, go to this website.
https://go.fitzgeraldpublishing.com/opt-in-page-youtube

Or use your phone to take a picture of this QR code, and it will take you to the Website for your Gift.

Inside the book, you will discover:

- **3000 Prompts** To help you make even more money online.
- **Save time:** You can search for new topics to create content on ChatGPT.
- **Expand knowledge:** Our Package of ChatGPT Prompts covers various topics, from science and technology to art and culture.

If you want to make even more money online, grab this free PDF.

Wait, that's not all; just for buying this book and getting the free PDF above, you can also earn another free Book.

You can use your phone to take a picture of this QR code.

Use the latest AI techniques to uncover online innovation's future. Take advantage! "Beyond ChatGPT and 50 New AI Tools: The Ultimate Guide to Discovering Cutting-Edge AI Tools Beyond ChatGPT" offers endless possibilities. Explore a variety of cutting-edge AI solutions to transform your work. Discover advanced AI tools beyond ChatGPT on this thrilling voyage.

Grab this free book if you want to make even more money online.

Introduction

Hi there, and welcome to endless possibilities with YouTube Social Media Marketing. My name is Blake Preston, and with the help of Brian Fitzgerald and Fitzgerald Publishing, I will teach you to exponentially grow your business and increase revenue using YouTube.

YouTube dominates the vast, ever-changing internet video landscape. YouTube has transformed the video business from its 2005 founding as a site to post personal videos to its status as the world's second-largest search engine and a vital tool for corporations, artists, and influencers.

Consider the effect's astonishing magnitude. YouTube has about two billion unique, logged-in users monthly. YouTube viewership exceeds 1 billion hours daily. Among these staggering figures is an opportunity to do what you care about, express what you think, promote what you offer, or tell a story that matters.

This book aims to be your YouTube trip buddy and the

complete guide. This book is for everyone interested in YouTube, whether they're aspiring video creators, companies looking to build their audience, or curious about the medium.

Consider Why YouTube is Revolutionary:

YouTube isn't only for kids and techies. It attracts all ages, backgrounds, and nations. This implies that even specialized content may be interesting.

Others who use YouTube as a creative outlet make money on it. This book teaches you how to monetize your content using ads, sponsorships, and more.

Personal Growth and Education YouTube has endless knowledge on every topic. This makes it a great teaching tool. When you start generating YouTube videos, you join a community of creators with different perspectives.

On any road, challenges are expected. The site's magnitude may intimidate some users. How can you be heard in the noise? How do you ensure your work reaches the right audience? How do you navigate YouTube's features?

Why You Should Read This Book.

We discuss YouTube's numerous aspects in the first chapter. This section offers project history and operations, which is crucial before starting.

Section 2 focuses on the foundation. Like a structure, your

YouTube channel needs a solid foundation, which involves researching your audience and creating a unique personality. Use this section as a map to stay on track.

Section 3 covers YouTube's mainstay: video creation. From the definition of outstanding content through filming and editing, this part covers making your content stand out.

Successful channel management is covered in Section 4. Learn these ways to boost content visibility, engagement, and conversions.

Section 5 concludes with commercialization. Following one's passion and gaining money aren't mutually incompatible. Follow the procedures in this section to optimize YouTube profits.

This handbook is also a guide, resource, and incentive. As we go into YouTube, remember that every YouTuber, from the most successful to the newest, started with the same goal: to share something. This voyage's limits are unknown if you're well-equipped.

Enjoy your YouTube experience. Start this journey with me.

SECTION 01

Understanding YouTube

In this age of immediate information and ever-changing social media landscapes, YouTube has become a staple of internet media. It combines TV, cinema, and the internet so everyone can voice their ideas. To truly utilize YouTube, one must first understand its intricate design.

YouTube: A Future, Present, and Past Time Machine

Let's revisit February 2005. Ex-PayPal employees Chad Hurley, Steve Chen, and Jawed Karim created YouTube. They laid the groundwork for a digital empire without knowing it.

"Me at the Zoo," uploaded by Jawed Karim in 2004, is considered YouTube's first video. It was brief—18 seconds of Karim discussing elephant trunks. This marked a new era of information delivery.

Today, YouTube has changed drastically. After Google bought it in November 2006, it soared from obscurity to global fame. YouTube receives billions of views daily and posts over 500 hours of video each minute, indicating its unparalleled influence on modern business, entertainment, and society.

YouTube's future seems brighter. YouTube's viewership and content diversity will likely expand as internet access and digital device use spread worldwide and younger, more acclimated generations become vital customers.

Video Development for YouTube

YouTube's variety and quality have grown over time. Once dominated by raw, unedited content, the site hosts feature films, documentaries, debate shows, and music videos.

The creative community has grown from amateurs sharing home videos to professionals with studios. YouTube is a top destination for short videos, serials, and documentaries.

The Future of YouTube

YouTube goes beyond keeping up with technology. With VR180 (which enables producers to record VR films with standard cameras) and YouTube Shorts (which competes with short videos), the platform is continually evolving.

Advanced analytics tools and AI are coming to enhance user experience and ad environments. As traditional TV and internet streaming merge, YouTube will be crucial.

Using YouTube to Network

YouTube is essential to social media discussions. Video makes YouTube more immersive and entertaining than text or photos.

The video's comment section allows debates and comments. Like, share, and subscribe enable users to engage with material and writers. YouTube is social because of this uploader-viewer interaction.

YouTube for Search Engines

YouTube is the second-largest search engine behind Google, yet this needs to be addressed. This distinguishes the platform for creators, companies, educators, and marketers.

When trying to "learn how" or "find out about," individuals prefer videos over text. We'll cover YouTube's search algorithm later, but for now, know that bringing suitable videos to the right viewers is crucial.

YouTube Search System

Anyone who wants to be seen on YouTube must learn its search tools. YouTube's algorithm is secret; however, a few factors impact a video's search ranking.

How well the video's title, description, and substance match the user's search is "relevant." Videos with more views, comments, and shares rank higher in search results. Video Length: Longer videos perform higher on YouTube's search results. The software also considers watching and searching histories.

Important Additional Information

A video's exposure and success depend on several things beyond the original search. The suggested video's sidebar boosts video visibility. Getting mentioned here can boost page views. Titles and thumbnails create first impressions. Attractive images and clear titles can increase click-through rates.

Investigation of YouTube is Activity #1.

Apply the fundamentals in a practical exercise. YouTube for downtime. Find what interests you. The most notable results—how are their names, photos, and descriptions? Participate systemically. Comment on a video, share it, or see some recommendations. Examine a popular channel in your profession. In what respects are they successful? Write this down.

This activity will familiarize you with the site and give input for future material.

Here's how to navigate YouTube's massive ecosystem. But this is only the start. Later chapters will teach you how to navigate this terrain and be noticed.

CHAPTER 01

What You Need to Know Before Getting Started

Suppose you will invest the next few months and years in establishing your brand on the YouTube platform. In that case, it makes sense to learn a little about the platform's origins and what makes it so unique. For example, did you know YouTube started as a dating platform? Few people know this, but co-founder Steven Chen said it was initially designed for dating so people could upload videos of themselves talking about their dream partner.

In this chapter, we will cover a bit of YouTube's history, present, and future, as well as why it's a social platform search engine. We will also get technical by introducing you to the robust YouTube algorithm so you can create your channel and content with the understanding necessary to help your videos perform well.

YouTube is a unique social networking platform for this simple reason. It's both a social networking channel and a search engine. So, it falls into the social media category, yet it's also far grander if you think about it. But how did it become this big giant? Indeed, it's not just because the Internet giant Google owns it. Right, you are! This is why it's best to start with an overview of YouTube's past, present, and future to align yourself with this ever-growing social and search engine platform.

YouTube: The Past, The Present, And The Future

Few people know this, but YouTube came due to a combined effort from three former PayPal employees. Chad Hurley, Steven Chen, and Jawed Karim believed that ordinary people would enjoy sharing personal homemade videos. So, they created the first website version of what we know today in early February 2005. The beta version was launched in May 2005 and already started attracting 30,000 visitors daily. Yes, that was a massive number at the time. By its official launch in December 2005, the platform had over two million video views daily. By January 2006, those numbers had increased to more than 25 million views. A few months later (March 2006), the platform had over 25 million uploaded videos, with over 20,000 uploaded daily. Even back then, these were huge numbers. The platform has shown no signs of slowing down since its launch.

Regarding funding, the founders got their first actual funding in November 2005 from Sequoia Capital, which invested more than $3 million. Of course, with the massive growth I just shared, it wasn't too long before popularity took over, and

Google decided it was time to take their lion's share. In November 2006, Google bought YouTube for a cool $1.65 billion. Yes, that was a B (billion), not a million.

Fast forward years of successful growth, more popularity, and many stardom case studies from YouTube creators who gained fame and fortune, YouTube has yet to show any signs of slowing down. But their early days were rather humble. In the early days, YouTube was very "homely" and raw. You'd find hilarious pranks, videos showing interesting locations, crazy stunts, and neighborhood entertainment. There were only square videos available at that time. But with time, the platform matured and expanded to include political debates, unfiltered war footage, musical performances, instructional videos, and lots more comedy and entertainment. In 2007, YouTube partnered with CNN to create an opportunity for ordinary citizens to interact with potential United States presidential candidates, exponentially increasing the platform's engagement.

Video Progress on YouTube

As I mentioned, the first video ever published was titled "**Me at The Zoo**." Since then, YouTube has gone from zero to 1 billion views in under a decade. According to Statista, YouTube currently has 2 billion users worldwide and is growing. (Statista, 2019). It, therefore, stands to be the most prominent social network - even more significant than Facebook.

Many still consider it the most accessible platform to share video content with a broad audience. Setting up a channel and getting started is fast and straightforward, as you'll learn in an upcoming section. With a good strategy, you can be unknown today and reach millions of views worldwide by the end of the week.

You can easily reach people of any age group today on YouTube because research shows that young and older people using the Internet also watch videos on YouTube. Since most people prefer to consume visual content, the growth of YouTube and your ability to succeed are unlimited. But what about in the future? What are some of the predictions being made?

The Future of YouTube

Video is still expected to remain front and center in our society. It has become the most effective strategy anyone can use to connect with an audience. You don't even need fancy equipment or a professional studio to do so.

Many smartphone users find engaging video content challenging to resist, which will continue to be the case. Why? Because according to recent data, 85% of Internet users in the U.S. watch video content. And in 2021, the average person is expected to spend 100 minutes daily watching online videos! That's a 19% increase since 2019.

While it's hard for anyone to accurately prophecy where any of these social networking platforms will be in another decade, there is enough reason to assume YouTube will only go for a while. There's a strong chance that today's YouTubers will become tomorrow's moguls. The Internet and the digital economy are still in their infancy. We know the best is yet to come, and those who learn to ride this wave with YouTube might continue to experience tremendous success regardless of the new adaptations the platform brings about.

Consider people like PewDiePie (Felix Kjellberg). He is arguably the most famous YouTuber on the planet, generating billions of views from his channel. With all the fame and money he's acquired over the years, it's unlikely he would sizzle out quickly. In fact, according to an interview with The Guardian Magazine a while back, PewDiePie hinted that he's contemplating expanding into creating a multi-channel network at some point. There's a good chance many of these YouTubers who have become influencers are more likely to seek out television stardom or even develop their networks. Imagine any future you'd like, and I can assure you YouTube can become a vehicle for that accomplishment.

As for the platform itself, given that its parent company is Internet Goliath Google, it will continue to evolve, adapt, and invest in further growth within the forum.

When the platform launched, it only had square videos and no advertising opportunities. Over the years, it has evolved and expanded to include a very robust advertising system. The video formats have also been growing. It's wise for every YouTuber to keep up with these ever-changing video requirements. As an overview, YouTube allows you to upload sizes ranging from

240p to 2160p(4K).

- 240p: 426x240 pixels
- 360p: 640x360 pixels
- 480p: 854x480 pixels
- 720p: 1280x720 pixels
- 1080p: 1920x1080 pixels
- 1440p: 2560x1440 pixels
- 2160p: 3840x2160 pixels

If you're learning his stuff, you can upload a video as tiny as 426X240 pixels or go as large as 3840X2160 pixels. But dimension is one of many things you need to get right. You must also consider video size, length, and aspect ratio, especially now that they have added new features such as vertical video stories.

We will dive deeper into the different video sizes available, whether you're running ads or posting organically for your channel, so stay tuned for those fresh updates and features in an upcoming chapter. For now, realize that it will be essential to use the recommended video size and keep refreshing yourself on the latest changes. Why?

If you want to attract more views and profit, use the correct YouTube video size. Failure to do so will result in low-quality content, repelling the audience you're looking to attract. Therefore, please regularly visit the Content Creator Academy webpage, which has all things YouTube-related.

YouTube As A Social Media Platform

Do you know why YouTube is considered a social media platform? To answer that effectively, let's clarify an online social network. An online social network is a platform where you and other like-minded people can connect. You can build relationships, exchange and share information, etc. YouTube is a platform that enables you to do all that and so much more. Not only can you build new connections, but you can also learn from new people who are halfway across the world from you. When a social network is done right, it becomes a thriving ecosystem where content creators, brands, and users benefit from actively engaging on the platform. I'd say YouTube has done a fantastic job creating such an environment.

One of the critical factors to consider when labeling YouTube as a social media platform comes from this simple word - community.

There is a massive community on YouTube of people producing, sharing, and consuming content. The platform's most active and engaged people feel part of something more significant, as they belong. These people support each other, hang out together, and share common values. That, my friend, is called community building. It may not be a community in the traditional offline sense of the word where everyone is physically next to each other, but it is, nonetheless.

Because YouTube is a social media platform, more is needed to occasionally post videos and pray to the traffic gods that your channel will attract people. Focusing solely on data and getting views on your video could be better. The approach should be the same as any other social networking site. It would be best to focus on connecting with and interacting with the people you wish to have as part of your YouTube community. We will talk more in-depth about how to do this, but it is essentially about posting quality videos with content your ideal audience will find valuable. Like other social channels, you can send out friend requests, ask people to subscribe to your channel and engage in live chats, especially when you do live streaming. More on that later.

The other thing I love about YouTube is that you can create honest conversations around your video content. Since most people spend a lot of time watching videos on the platform, if you engage and interact with community members by asking questions on the comments and making sure you reply to all the comments people make, you can demonstrate to your new audience that you care. And they, in turn, will follow and consume what you offer. The more value and engagement you bring to this social network, the more success you will experience, especially as a business owner.

YouTube As a Search Engine Platform

A while back, Google (the parent company that owns YouTube) released a resource that answers many of the questions we all ask when we decide to set up a YouTube channel. Namely, how exactly does YouTube work?

While I'm sure they didn't spill all their secrets, they have given us enough knowledge to leverage to our advantage. In a later chapter, I will discuss the YouTube algorithm and hacks to help you rank higher on their search engine. But to get the most out of that conversation, you must understand that YouTube is a search engine like Google, Yahoo, etc. There's a tremendous amount of organic traffic to be enjoyed within YouTube's platform because many people use that search bar. Besides that fact, we also have the added benefit of being favored highly by Google when they rank content on the homepage. Videos from YouTube consistently rank high on a Google search page, and I don't know if you noticed, but Google added a new tab specifically titled "video." So, when doing the regular search, people are still being served video results for their queries. Let me put this practically for you so you can understand the power of this.

Suppose your potential client is looking for a service you can offer. They head over to Google and type in their query. Millions of results show up in the form of regular articles. But they see a tab "video" and click on that because, let's face it, most people prefer to watch than read. Videos are more saturated than text-based solutions. Since you're smart, you have a video explainer showing them exactly how to solve their need and how you do it fast and affordable. What are the chances of getting that cold lead and converting a customer? I'd say high. You don't need a big audience or a huge channel. What you need is to understand how to leverage YouTube.

How YouTube Search Works

The search ranking system on YouTube is fantastic because it sorts through over 500 hours of content uploaded every minute. Then, it finds the most relevant results for the search query given by the end-user. Thanks to Google's information, we know you need to focus on three main elements: quality, relevance, and engagement.

Quality:

That refers to how authoritative your channel and content are for the target audience. YouTube wants expert, traditional, and trustworthy content for its community members. That's why I always recommend starting narrow with a specific topic. It's much easier to prove that your channel is worth being promoted when you focus on delivering quality content on what you know well. The more you can provide that, the better your videos will perform.

Relevance:

YouTube's algorithm is still a mystery, even for expert hackers.

But what we all know for sure is that being relevant is a critical factor for channel growth. There are many indicators the algorithms look for to determine whether something is relevant to an audience or not, some of which include the video content itself (though not 100% perfect), title, description, and tags.

Engagement:

The last thing I want us to discuss here that the algorithm cares about is video engagement. Watch time is especially critical for the algorithm because it uses that as a key indicator of whether to continue promoting your content. The more people watch and stay on the platform thanks to your video, the more they will promote your stuff to a bigger audience.

Other Factors That Are a Must-Know

In the earlier report, YouTube shared that they care a lot about promoting authoritative content from reliable sources. But only when it is appropriate. So, when it comes to scientific, political, medical information, or breaking news, they will promote the most credible channels and personalities on the platform.

The critical thing to take away from this is to build credibility. You do not have to be Oprah or CNBC, but you do need to demonstrate to the algorithm that your content can be trusted. This is especially true if you are dealing with educational type of content. This may apply less to entertainment or music channels because what matters most in such cases is popularity, freshness, and relevancy, which we already discussed.

Recommended videos

This is exciting because it offers us an opportunity to do well immediately. Have you ever noticed the "recommended" icon when watching content on YouTube? You can usually see it in your dashboard's "Up Next" section. This is YouTube's way of suggesting what you should consume next. The algorithm factors in many things before making that recommendation, including the channels you're subscribed to, your watch history, the time of day, etc. Getting your video to appear on this recommended list will significantly accelerate your channel growth. I even have hacks that will increase your chances of appearing on that suggestions list.

Before we can move on, I'd also like to emphasize that YouTube does factor in personalization when determining what to show a user. If you've noticed how many times recommended videos show up based on your recent activity, this will make sense. As a YouTube user, your interface gets populated by more things you've watched, liked, and interacted with. Flip perspective for a bit and think like a creator. The more you can create content that a user interacts with, the more of your stuff YouTube will serve them. Therefore, it is imperative to create content with your ideal consumer in mind. You want to create content you feel confident they will want to click on, watch, and like. That's your golden ticket to the success you desire on this platform.

Want to Get More Technical About How the YouTube Algorithm Works?

If what I just shared needs to be more sophisticated for you, I've got something that will satisfy the tech geek in you. There's a research paper published by Google engineers Paul Covington, Jay Adams, and Emre Sargin. They break down the signals they use to rank videos for YouTube recommendations. If you can recall, recommendations are a huge deal when getting more people to know about your channel. In the paper, they talk about the following:

1. Click-through rate. That refers to the likelihood of someone clicking on your video after seeing it.

2. Watch time. That refers to the total time viewers spend watching your videos.

3. How many videos the user has watched from your channel?

4. Recently, the user watched a video about the same topic.

5. What the user has searched for in the past.

6. The users previously watched videos.

7. The user's demographic information and location.

Want to read the entire research paper (Deep Neural Networks for YouTube Recommendations)? Check out the resource section for links.

Activity #1: Exploring YouTube

Now, it's time to start taking some action. Before getting into the next chapter, it's good to familiarize yourself with this platform through the lens of the new insights and lessons learned. So here's what you're going to do.

Open an incognito webpage, sign into your personal YouTube if you have one, and start browsing. First, begin by entering the homepage and playing around with the search bar at the top. Type in a query around your topic of expertise or whatever your channel will be about. Observe how many search results come up. Notice which top channels are being promoted and look at their titles, video length, number of views, year of publication, and quality of the content. You should also check the sidebar menu and notice what YouTube recommends. Browse the platform from the eyes of a consumer, your potential subscriber.

Before moving on, the last activity is to type in the same search query on the main Google search tab and then hover over "videos." Notice how many videos you encountered on YouTube show up here. What you learn from exploring YouTube through this new lens will equip you as you move forward.

CHAPTER 02

Why YouTube?

By now, it should be evident that YouTube is on fire. Billions of users log in every month to consume content. There are also as many content creators or YouTubers in the backend, pushing out hundreds of content every minute of the day. The amount of activity taking place on this platform can feel quite overwhelming. The fact that you can find almost any topic on any genre can make one wonder why they should even consider setting up a channel. Everything is already there.

Yes and no. There's a lot of content on any topic you might have in mind. Still, the reality is you are a unique individual. Even if you start a channel with a common issue, as long as you remain true to yourself, it won't be like any other channel because no one can imitate you. That is what makes YouTube unique. There's enough room for every content creator. Your only obstacle is figuring out how to be more of yourself so your content stands out.

The question you need to ask isn't why I should invest my time, resources, and energy on YouTube when over 500 hours of video are uploaded every minute. Instead, it should be a question directed at your self-expression as a unique human being. Meaning - what am I highly passionate about that I can also become an authoritative voice for?

Most people who start a channel do so out of sheer passion and an urge to share their message, but that's not the only reason to become a YouTuber. You could also do it because you want to become famous like the Kardashians or to generate income. There shouldn't be a wrong or right reason, but there should be a big enough reason.

Always start by identifying your "why" for creating a successful channel because you will need the fuel when the going gets tough. So here are some of the reasons I know of for starting a YouTube channel:

- For Passion, to express yourself to the world.
- For money.
- For fame.

For Passion

If you want to use this platform to express yourself and share your passions with the world, you're not alone. Many of the channels that have successfully grown to millions of followers were created by YouTubers who had a power they wanted to share with an audience. To do the same, the first thing you must do is identify what your passions and talents are.

What's real and proven about creating a passion-based YouTube channel is that you can go right. Passion always drives success. In the world of content creation, knowing how long and how much effort is required to grow a thriving channel, your passion is the fuel that will keep you going until things start to snowball. Consider this for a moment. Have you ever been given a task or project you disliked or didn't care about? Can you recall how laborious and lengthy the process was? Perhaps you procrastinated, quit, then un-quit several times over, and it was an experience you couldn't wait to finish.

Now, think about when you got to work on a project you love. How enjoyable was that experience? You probably skipped meals, worked overtime including weekends, and even forgo your weekend Netflix Binge-watching just because of how immersed you were. Your YouTube content creation and channel management should resemble the second example. How do you do this? Let me share a simple process to help you identify a topic you are passionate about. Once you pin that down and it feels right, every other choice will revolve around that passion.

How to Discover Your Passion and Turn It Into Video Content for YouTube.

Open your Google Docs or Word document, and let's carry out an exercise to help you identify your passion. Remember, this exercise should be fun. Don't overthink things. Write anything and everything that comes to mind because there is no right or wrong. If nothing comes, make something up.

Ask yourself this question - What do I love doing and talking about? Example answer: I love running in nature, cooking, traveling, reading comic books, painting, hiking, and writing poetry.

Answer this question - I can spend hours reading, researching, thinking, and learning about...X...[fill in your blank]. Example answer: I can spend hours reading, researching, thinking, learning about comic books, and creating characters.

Write down all the activities you've enjoyed. Go back as far as you can and list everything down. Example answer: Selling lemonade when I was nine, drawing manga as a teen, playing piano, cooking, painting with watercolors, juggling, writing comedy, etc. Anything and everything you've enjoyed doing should go on this list, whether you did it a year ago or ten years ago.

Write down all your strengths, skills, and any work experience you've had. Make sure these are practical. For example, answer social media manager, sales representative, party planner, florist, etc.

What are some of your personality traits that people say they like about you? Three qualities that people have mentioned make you unique. They must be positive traits; if you don't know, text a few friends now and ask them to share with you. Example answer: Funny, resilient, and confident.

Pick and choose, and then put in some research time. Pick the top three topics or activities that stand out from your list and order them in priority. The one with the most electrifying energy is the one you should start researching most.

Researching in this context means heading to the YouTube search bar and typing in the chosen topics. See what comes up. How much content has been created around your passion? Are people engaging, commenting, and liking existing content? What quality is the content? Which titles are performing best? Click on the channels with the content you're passionate about and notice how that channel is set up. I recommend getting a Google Chrome extension like VidIQ or Keywords Everywhere if you'd like to see exact metrics and volume searches. These are great for helping you figure out what keywords and content are performing well at high volume and low competition.

The purpose of doing research is to ensure you're going after an interest that has an existing and engaged audience. Most people say YouTube needs to be more saturated, and there is still time to start a channel. I'm afraid I strongly must disagree. Now is the best time to start your track, and you can grow it even faster than the rest of us because you get to ride the wave of success we've already created.

By finding channels posting on the topic you're passionate

about, you can get ideas of content topics that work. You also get to see the mistakes they are making or the gaps still need to be filled. You will also feel what the audience cares about and what they want to see more of. So, if you find competition around your topic, get excited because you're on the right path, and I will show you strategies to leverage this competition.

Now that you've identified your passion and validated that there's an audience for that topic, it's time to start thinking of content you can post. If you still need to identify what you love, don't worry. Here are some more questions that will help.

1. If you could be remembered for three things after you're gone from this life, what would you want those three to be?

2. What would you do with your time if money wasn't an issue and you had financial freedom?

3. What is one thing your friends and family usually come to you to ask for advice or a recommendation? Make sure it's something you also enjoy helping them out with.

For Money

Some people start their YouTube channel because they hear of the many YouTubers making a full-time income and traveling the world. There are also countless stories of content creators who have started a side hustle of YouTube content creation and generated more passive income than their primary job salary.

For example, I have a friend who was employed as a customer service rep in a furniture company. He decided to test his ability to succeed on YouTube and generate passive income by teaching arts and crafts, DIY sessions, and promoting unique furniture pieces. His channel now earns him about $15k in passive income each month, more than his salary at the store. So, if you've been wondering how to make a side income or even want to be a full-time YouTuber traveling the world and creating fantastic content about the cool places you're exploring, this can be a great way to fund that lifestyle.

Many consider YouTube to be the king of the side hustle. Why? Here are some reasons worth knowing if you want to increase your income. YouTube monetization is very consistent and can be very lucrative if you have the right strategy. In a later section, we will talk about different monetization methods. For now, realize that as a content creator on YouTube, you will have the opportunity to generate income on your channel.

They're recurring and evergreen income possibilities on YouTube. What do I mean by this? You can create a video this week and, three years from now, still make money from it. I noticed some similarities after interviewing many YouTubers and plotting my success on the platform. A key one that stands out is that video creation has been happening for years. Years ago, no one knew us when we started making the videos. If we were lucky, video views ranged from a few hundred to a few thousand, but we kept creating awesome videos.

I can tell you there was no income coming in for any of us. I certainly never made a dime. But I kept persisting. After a few years, I noticed my growth started to gain momentum, and then slowly, a few thousand views turned into a few hundred thousand. By then, the subscriber count was decent enough, and each video's earnings increased. Ultimately, a good, steady income becomes a reality. I've heard this from almost every fellow creator I've interviewed, with just a few exceptions. All this to say, you can do it, but you need to play the long game. And the best part about YouTube is the more mature your channel becomes. The better you'll be rewarded by your older content if you didn't take shortcuts initially.

Suppose you're looking for a side hustle or want a lifestyle funded entirely by your content creation. In that case, YouTube is excellent for helping you accomplish this. And as I shared with you, I know many people who earn more from their YouTube than their 9 to 5.

For Fame

Want to become YouTube famous? It's not too late, but you need to be prepared to put in the work. Being a YouTube favorite has become a real thing. It is considered just as substantial as being a rock star. Of course, it's more challenging than it used to be, but it's still possible.

If you want to become a social media influencer or grow a brand, YouTube is a great platform to help you create fame.

Nowadays, some famous YouTubers have the same special treatment as TV celebrities. Have you noticed? I have seen comedians, musicians, and other entertainers jumpstart their careers by being "discovered" on YouTube. Even Justin Beiber first started on YouTube. So, whether you want to grow a personal or company brand or become a well-known social media celebrity, YouTube can make that happen.

But before you get too excited, let's ensure you set realistic expectations. You may think YouTube will make you a celebrity overnight. There was a time when it could happen, but given how mature the platform has become, it will take a lot more strategic thinking and effort.

When YouTube first started, platform tools like the video response tool could be leveraged to gain a new audience's attention. You could piggyback on the rise and success of a YouTube star just by directly engaging in their hit videos using the video-response tool. This option no longer exists.

There's also the opportunity to collaborate with other successful YouTubers. That could help you get in front of a vast audience and go from zero to famous in a day, but unfortunately, a lot of work goes into creating these collaborations nowadays.

There must be a real-world connection. The more prominent stars are increasingly difficult to access if one is just getting started. Besides, even if someone has a big audience, they can still subscribe to your channel. And then, of course, there is the growing issue of creating high-quality videos with graphics, excellent studio lighting, scenery, etc. Top creators already have the financing, resources, and support from the partner program and other sponsorships, but when you're just starting, all you have is a webcam in your bedroom or living room. It will take a while before people start to respect and admire what you do. But if you keep persisting, it is possible.

Activity #2: Finding Your Motivation

It's time to implement what you've just learned in this chapter. If you want to become successful with your YouTube endeavor, you need to know what drives you. What is causing you to start this channel? What's your big "WHY" for this? The bigger the way, the more likely you are to persist and succeed. To do this, here are some questions to answer.

1. What is my goal for this YouTube channel?

2. Why am I choosing that goal as my primary goal?

3. How far am I willing to stretch to make the goal a reality?

4. What is my vision for myself if I consider where I want to be two years from now?

5. What is the vision for the channel? I.e., what do I want it to represent?

6. Why is the success of this channel so vital to me now?

7. How will my life change when I hit the goals I have set for this YouTube channel?

SECTION 02

Your YouTube Channel

Your channel is your shop in YouTube's rising economy. It's when individuals learn about you and your brand's benefits. Whether you want to educate, entertain, inspire, or all three, how you build and manage your channel may make or break it. Let's begin creating a meaningful channel.

Focus Attention

Find your channel's specialty before filming or designing a great logo. Without your YouTube channel's basement, the building may fall.

Find your market by picking a niche. Content producers often use "niche" as a buzzword. It denotes a small yet significant market segment. Discovering your YouTube specialty is like finding the sweet spot where your hobbies and audience demands meet.

A target market may help you focus. It enables personalization, audience analysis, and sticking out in a crowded medium.

Encouraging individuals to watch specialty channels helps them meet others with similar interests.

The way to find your target market. Ask yourself: What matters? Which talks or activities keep you interested in hours? Checking Competition: Anyone Else Making This Content? Does this target anyone? Use YouTube's suggested searches and Google Trends. Identifying Need: Do you know your market's information gaps? Perhaps you found your way in.

Competency Assessment

What Are You Contributing? Target Market Characterization: Identify your ideal reader. Consider their demographics to create appealing content. A/B and Iterative Improvement First, make some videos, then observe how people react. Don't be afraid to change. Stay focused on your specialty. Building audience trust demands consistent, high-quality content.

Knowing Your Audience

You've chosen an audience for your work. Knowing your audience is as vital as learning your topic. Despite appearances, studying rivals might help you understand your target market. Your niche's successful channels will have done the work for you. Their articles, audience engagement rates, and comments may teach you a lot.

Shortlist the top channels for your profession. Use these recommendations to proceed. Check its contents: Think the scope is what? How are their videos structured? They update material how often?

Check their involvement: Which videos got the most reactions? This may reveal your target market's priorities. Join the comment feedback loop. Viewers often propose changes or additional content. This info is helpful.

Naming and Branding Your Channel

Building a channel brand requires more than a logo and name. Your audience's feelings, thoughts, and actions are in reaction to your content and their group identity.

Make your video stand out from the crowd online. Uniformity builds audience trust and devotion. Community: Brands can make viewers feel like they belong. The Basics of YouTube Channel Creation Your channel name should represent your videos' tone and be memorable.

Your logo and banner symbolize your brand. Consider utilizing fonts, colors, and pictures that match your writing style. Channel summary: Summary of what to expect. Search engine optimization keywords can also be added naturally. Channel Promo: Like your network's teaser. A captivating video that summarizes your persona and work in minutes.

YouTube allows you to customize your channel's homepage to highlight your content. You may organize and prioritize audience content using playlists, highlighted videos, and other channel sections.

In conclusion, your YouTube channel represents your passion, dedication, and goal of providing value to your audience. Establishing a channel identity, understanding its audience, and providing content that connects will help you attract and retain viewers. We'll study content development science to keep your channel full of relevant, entertaining videos.

CHAPTER 03

Determine Your Focus

As we gain momentum on this quest to become a highly successful income-producing YouTuber, it's time to turn your focus on delivering value. What can you bring to the platform that will cause others to pay attention, engage with your content, and become loyal subscribers? To help you answer that question effectively and efficiently, we will break down how you can pick or decide on a niche. I'll also share with you the best types of niches that are performing well. But before we get to that, perhaps you're wondering why picking a niche is essential.

I've been in heated conversations with intelligent business owners who wondered the same thing. Creatives need help understanding that marketing to everyone means you're marketing to no one. Recently, I was introduced to a life and health coach who was in the process of starting his YouTube channel. He wants to become an authority on the platform and attract hot leads that can easily convert into paying customers, and he wants that to happen fast. When I asked what his niche would be, he hesitated and said, "I want to help billions of people, so I don't want to limit myself by being so narrow with a niche topic."

That, my friend, is the recipe for YouTube's failure, especially now that it has matured. The best-performing channels are super niched. And you know why? Because when you focus on one vertical, you become known as the industry leader, the credible resource, and the go-to person for that topic. When new potential subscribers and future buyers come across your content and immediately understand the problem you can solve for them, they are more likely to stick around, engage, connect, and convert. When you focus on one niche, you have clarity, and people love clarity.

It also makes your channel more memorable. Can you imagine how Coca-Cola would be if they had started advertising soft drinks, shoes, and food years ago? Building the fortified brand we've all grown accustomed to would have been extra hard. Everyone sees that red label on a soft drink or Santa holding a bottle, and we immediately think - Coca-Cola.

You don't have deep pockets and years of branding budget to waste, so please save yourself by focusing on a niche. Bring as much clarity and simplicity to your new audience as possible so they quickly associate you with the result you offer.

Picking A Niche

How, then, does one determine a niche for their new channel? In the case of the life and health coach I mentioned above, he could talk about mindset, lifestyle, working out, healthy eating, nutrition, and the list goes on and on. While he can always create content around any of these significant categories once his channel gains momentum, it is best to focus on one vertical when just starting. But which one first?

You may need help determining your niche or have too many options. Regardless, we can still help you figure out the perfect place. To start, go back to the answers from previous chapters. The exercises you've been doing so far are a foundation for this exercise because now you understand more about yourself and why you want this channel. Now, it's time to dive deeper. We need to find that sweet spot between gained knowledge about ourselves and what we know about our ideal audience. In other words, the overlap between what you love (what you're passionate about) and what your ideal audience wants is the sweet spot for your content. That becomes your niche topic.

Steps to Selecting Your Niche

Review Your Strengths and Skills

The first step is detailing how you've been most helpful to others throughout your career. Suppose you're coming out of college and think about what friends usually come to you for help with. Again, I want you to write the answers down. What skills have you developed? What leading roles and responsibilities have you had? What primary benefits did you deliver in the parts you've had? What successes have you had? Make sure to be super specific here.

Map Out Your Ideal Audience and What They Need.

It's imperative to identify what your ideal audience considers valuable and what needs they have that you can fulfill. You must create a detailed audience persona profile to help you figure out this puzzle piece. Here are some of the questions to answer for that persona profile.

- •Whom would you love to work with?
- What shared values do you have with this person?
- What makes them unique?
- Why does this person come to YouTube? What are they looking to experience?
- What are their goals and ambitions?
- What are their current challenges and worries?
- What is their purchase behavior? For example, they research online but like to buy offline.
- What is a pain or problem or lack they are experiencing as it relates to what your channel can offer?

Research to See if There's a Demand for Your Identified Topic.

Now that you've found that sweet spot between what you love and what your audience needs, it's time to head over to YouTube and see how much demand there is for your topic. We do this to ensure people want to watch your content type.

To conduct this research effectively, you need to write down keywords from your chosen topic or some titles you would make a video about. Then, type in that title or those keywords on the YouTube search to see what comes up. If there are a ton of results (millions of results), then I suggest getting more specific with that title. If there are zero results, no one may be looking for that type of content. What I recommend is to create content that is somewhere in between those two extremes.

Do Some Due Diligence for Income-Earning Potential.

Even though a topic is popular, it may be different for you, especially if you want to get rich. Many niches do well on the platform but earn the content creator little money. So, if you're going to make a lot of money through your channel, check to see income-earning potential. Find out if a company would be willing or likely to sponsor you to use their products or whether you can create a side business alongside your channel. Monetization is worth thinking about before settling on a niche. Sponsorship is very lucrative, but you need a good strategy; otherwise, it won't work.

Your channel must be aligned with the income avenue you wish to leverage most. For example, if you want to be paid by brands, research the brands that seem to be paying fellow YouTubers to create content. Most good creators always let their audience know when doing sponsored content, so that's a great way of getting some companies' names within your niche. If you're interested in sponsorship, make sure you have some offers to give your audience as they learn to trust you. Having this plan from the start ensures you'll make all the right choices, including niche picking.

Best Types of YouTube Niches

Not every niche can be monetized. The most popular ones work well; some are way easier than others. Here's a list of the most popular and easy-to-monetize niches.

- **How-to Tutorials**

This is the most popular and best niche on YouTube. Based on my experience, most people on this platform want to learn something. And since we all, at some point, need to know something, starting a channel that teaches "how-to" for your skill, talent, or passion seems like a great idea. It can also become very lucrative. Answering "how to..." questions can quickly build your audience and generate clients for your brand or business. Whether it's how to tie your unique shoelaces, how to clean your carpets, how to make specific floral arrangements for a particular occasion, how to get rid of a stain, or whatever else you do, you can quickly gather tens of thousands of not millions of views over time.

• **Animals**

Cute animals have been trending on YouTube since the beginning, and the trend hasn't slowed down. This niche is still popular, and given how trendy cat videos have become, you can consider getting into this niche if you love animals. That doesn't mean everyone with cats should start a YouTube channel.

Make sure it aligns with your brand and the objective of the channel. For example, a bakery should avoid getting into this niche! A vet should consider having a channel around cute animals. You can create content with animals doing funny things and center it on humor and entertainment. If you're more of an educational type, consider making videos on animal training, pet product reviews, and animal care.

• **Lifestyle**

Lifestyle has become one of the more popular niches on the platform. It's mainly because a lifestyle vlogger needs to fit neatly into a particular niche. So, their content can be wildly varied and carry differing undertones. Some lifestyle vloggers rely heavily on humor, sarcasm, drama, or gossip, giving their content an edge that people seem to love. Another thing about lifestyle vlogging is that it's incredibly personal. People usually disclose a lot of personal information about themselves, so if you lead a private life, there may be a better type of content for you.

• Food

Cooking and all things food-related are massive on YouTube. So, if you love cooking, eating, and critiquing food, you can create a successful channel with a vast audience. Show off amazing recipes, share some of the gadgets and tools you use in the kitchen, and you can't go wrong. Foodies are abundant on YouTube.

• Gaming

The most famous YouTubers are gamers. Correct me if I'm wrong, but some of these individuals have become real-world celebrities. PewDiePie, Jack Septiceye, Markiplier, and SSSniperWolf are just a few names that have gained global recognition. Why? Because these individuals have dominated YouTube. They are making tons of money doing what they love the most - gaming. You could be the same, but you must be fresh and different.

• Makeup

One of the most popular YouTube niches is makeup, so this is a great starting point if you're in the beauty space. And before you assume I am only talking about women's makeup, I'd like to point out that you could do well with men's makeup. Yes, you read me right. Even men want tutorials on how to do their makeup! Be forewarned, though; competition is fierce in this niche, but the audience is enormous and engaged.

• Fashion

Fashion is another popular niche on YouTube; you can approach it from various angles, even if you're not a designer. You can review clothing items, share styling tips, or start your fashion line if you're talented. This is one of the best and most accessible niches to get sponsors or even do affiliate marketing, which we will delve into later.

• Tech review

As we become a more tech-driven society, more and more people are coming to YouTube to watch tutorials or reviews on the latest tech and software products. Whether it's apps and software or physical hardware, you will have an audience if you can create engaging and valuable content. Are you good at helping others learn how to operate, assemble, or choose the right tech for their needs?

You can focus on workplace and productivity tech, home tech, or even small tech gadgets we carry daily. Your only limitation is your need for imagination and creativity.

• Sports

Are you a sports fanatic or maybe a former pro or amateur athlete? Then YouTube has an audience that would love your content. I have seen everything from sports vloggers to amateur reporters following around their favorite sports teams and sharing a different perspective with their audience than what professional journalists would share. And all these types of content do well. You don't have to be an officially appointed ambassador to create excellent content and keep your audience updated with the latest news. All you need is passion. Just be careful not to show copyrighted materials because that would lead to many unpleasant experiences with the authorities.

- **Photography**

Another popular niche is photography. Many budding photographers look to YouTube for sound advice on how to take better shots. You can offer tutorials on photography and the equipment you use. This can be an excellent channel for affiliate marketing opportunities.

- **Travel**

Who likes a great travel channel? Some of the sexiest YouTube channels I've come across are travel channels with great storytelling infused into them. A vast and starving audience is waiting for you if you love to travel the world and have fantastic stories to share. People love escaping reality or that horrid cubicle with a good travel video. It inspires, motivates, and uplifts travel enthusiasts. The best part is that many full-time YouTubers are digital nomads traveling the world and finding creative ways to cover their expenses to continue building their channel. If you dream of traveling the world, YouTube could be your golden ticket to seeing some of our planet's best-hidden gems and the wealthiest cultures.

• **Music**

Do you have a passion for music? Do you compose, sing, DJ, review, or teach others how to play an instrument? YouTube is an excellent platform for launching yourself. Some of the most viewed videos are music videos, and the best part is that you can go into any music genre, and you'll still get a decent audience size. I also know some channels that do commentaries on music news, give advice, report on the latest news from their favorite musicians, or even teach others how to play a particular instrument. Your options are endless regarding content types, and there's a healthy audience to support you.

• **ASMR**

ASMR, or Autonomous Sensory Meridian Response, has grown in recent years. It's all about the experience - using soothing sounds and imagery to relax viewers. ASMR content creators are all about taking their audience on a transformative journey through their sense organs.

And there you have it: the top niches on YouTube that are popular and easier to monetize. These niches already have audiences looking for content daily, so if you pick one, you are in luck. There's a ready-made audience for you, thanks to the work of your peers who launched before you. All you must do is develop the right plan to attract some of those engaged people to your channel.

Activity #3: Time To Choose

As you might have realized by now, each chapter must close with an implementation step. After going through the different exercises and discovering the top-performing niches, it's time to pick your niche.

Review your notes and come up with the top three niches that excite you the most. If you already know precisely the one to go for. But I encourage you to have more than one that you can start experimenting with for at least six weeks before settling on one. This is because I have seen many of my students get bored a few weeks into their content creation and give up on growing their channel.

Listen, you'll need to consistently create unique content for the next many years if you want to succeed at this. Therefore, you need to pick a niche that you are confident won't become a bore or burden 50 videos into it. That's why I suggest having more than one - but limited to three -different verticals and then creating content on each for a short while to see which one still excites you after a few weeks. It also allows you to see the audience response to test if one of them attracts more eyeballs and subscribers.

Pro tip:

When you make your choice, be sure to pick complementary

niches. For example, Lifestyle vlogging and photography can align well. If, after a few weeks, you realize lifestyle isn't for you, then it's lovely to focus on photography only. Now it's your turn. What niche will you choose?

CHAPTER 04

Understanding Your Audience

There are a lot of unhelpful myths surrounding the existing YouTube audience. It will serve you well to read and understand this chapter carefully, as it will impact your content strategy and channel growth moving forward.

Most people assume YouTube is for young single male personas or that only the younger demographics are active users. This is not accurate. According to a study conducted by Google and Nielsen, the average YouTube viewer is just as likely to be female as male. Young single Millenials being the only audience is also a myth because the same research said YouTube users have more potential to have kids than non-users.

Another report, by Cast from Clay, shared U.S. statistics about YouTube users and revealed data that proved men and women use YouTube equally. There's a robust usage of the platform across all age groups, so this isn't just a younger demographic platform like TikTok and others. You will find a healthy and active audience of 65-75-year-olds. Granted, they use the platform in different proportions than the 15-30-year-olds. Still, they are actively engaged nonetheless. The data from Cast from Clay shows 96% of users aged between 18 - 24 years, 95% of users aged between 25 - 34 years old, 90% of users aged between 35 - 44 years old, 85% of users aged between 45 - 54 years old, 79% of users aged between 55 - 64 years old, 66% aged between 65 - 75 years old and 51% users aged 75 and over. Keep in mind these statistics reflect US users only. What we can take away from this is that all kinds of YouTube users range from teenagers to retired. Even in the United Kingdom, the statistics remain steady, showing YouTube has a stronghold in every age group and demographic.

How does knowing these different types of YouTube viewers benefit you?

It's straightforward. You can have any channel you desire, and your ideal audience will be ready to embrace your brand. Remember, you can only become a video influencer with one to influence. Well, I have just proven to you that on YouTube, you can become an influencer at any age, for any demographic. The most important thing is to determine what audience your content will serve and then focus on understanding what your people want. It's not enough to create a persona based on shallow things like gender, location, age, and job title. You need to know your audience more deeply so they can immediately resonate with your channel.

Understanding Your Competition

If you're a beginner, this part will help you quickly determine what works and doesn't in your niche. It will also show you best practices, industry standards, and some benchmarks you can use to create a fantastic channel. Even if you've set up your channel, I still encourage you to consider this book section. It's where you can learn how to check existing and trending channels in your niche. The goal isn't to copy your competition but to learn from them and improve their work. That way, your young channel can shave off some mistakes and learning curves they had to go through. Let's walk through how to do this now.

Creating A Benchmark for Your Channel

Make sure to fire up your Google Doc or Word document to create your custom benchmark in this process. Make sure to document this as much as possible.

Step one: Find the Best-Performing Channels in Your Niche.

I recommend gathering the top five to ten preferred channels where you know your audience is hanging out. Need help finding your competition? Here's a simple exercise.

Do in-depth market research online to determine who is discussing the same topic or selling the same products and services you want. By now, you should have the primary keyword or niche topic you'll focus on. Put that keyword or key phrase on the main Google search bar to see what comes up. You'll see a list of websites and ads ranking for it, and if you click on the "video" tabs, you will see all the videos ranking on Google. This is great because it already shows you the channels competing with you. Record everything on your Google sheet and click the channels of these videos whenever one resonates with you so you can see how they've set up their entire YouTube channel.

You can also go to a software called Ubersuggest and type in each keyword. You'll get a downloadable report of all the websites ranking for that topic. Take the names of those sites and head over to the YouTube search bar to see what kind of content they have on their channel. If you realize some high-ranking websites need a better YouTube channel, that's great because that's the opportunity you need to seize. If you find a great channel with lots of engagement and high-quality content, add that to your list of competitors. You can also do the same thing on other social media channels like Twitter and Instagram, especially if your topic is popular on these other networks. Use hashtags to find the most engaged accounts and spy on their YouTube channels. Your goal is to have a comprehensive list of five to ten competitors. Then, move on to the next step.

Step Two: Take Note of The Following Metrics For all the Identified Competitive YouTube Channels.

- The Total Number of Subscribers on the Channel.
- Subscribers Change.
- The Total Number of Videos on the Entire Channel.

- Videos Change.
- Videos Table.
- Views Total.
- Views Change.
- View Subscriber Rate.
- Average Views Per Video.
- Engagement Rate.
- Average Engagement Per Video.
- Middle Favorites Per Video.
- Average Likes Per Video.
- Average Dislikes Per Video.
- Moderate Comments Per Video.

Granted, this will be a lot of manual work, especially if your competitors have created lots of video content on their channels. So, if you'd like some help with this process, consider using software such as SocialBlade, a free online tool that can help you track YouTube statistics more effortlessly. In the resources section, you will find all the tools I've recommended throughout this book.

Once you've gathered all this data, it's time to decide which benchmarks you will set for your channel. Allow that to influence the KPIs you'll put in the coming months. How will you know if your channel is doing well?

The data collected from channels in your niche can help you determine what a good audience engagement should be. You can continue using analytics to track growth month over month. The YouTube analytics dashboard will find many of those basic data sets. However, if you'd like something more robust to help you with analytics, consider investing in tools such as Tubular Intelligence, which allows you to see what's trending on YouTube and how your videos perform. You can also get BuzzSumo, which is quite popular nowadays and has a YouTube Analyzer. This tool can help you find the right keywords, get a list of the most popular videos for your niche, analyze specific videos, or keep an eye on competitor channels.

Find my Audience Tool

This is a new tool by "Think With Google" that I've played around with and found extremely useful. It will help you get an overview of where your audience might be hanging out on YouTube, which channels they are likely watching, and what they plan to buy.

Once on the site (https://www.thinkwithgoogle.com/-feature/findmyaudience), you can begin by taking a tour. A "Take a tour" tab in the top right corner walks you through how the site works. I recommend signing in with your Gmail so you can save the detailed information you gather. For example, I typed in "In-market" for my audience preference, then chose the sports and fitness categories.

I learned three YouTube audiences are researching or planning to purchase sports and fitness-related products or services. The three groups are fitness products and services, outdoor recreational equipment, and sporting goods. When I clicked on fitness products and services, I found the top YouTube channels people shopping for fitness products and services are likely to be watching. Jeff Nippard (2.14M), Body Project (1M+), Sydney Cummings (706K), and Muscle & Strength (816K) are the channel names that popped up.

The tool also revealed some of the top products and services most relevant to my audience, including Activewear, video games, etc. This is valuable information for someone setting up their fitness channel, wouldn't you agree?

Now, you can access the same so that your channel can reach the right audience with the right message and offers based on their preferences.

Activity #4: The Channels on Your Chosen Niche

It's time to implement all that we've learned. In this activity, you will complete researching between five to ten competitor channels using the tools I suggested.

Identify what makes these channels popular. Identify some gaps, if any, or think of what you could do differently and better. Read as many comments as possible to see how the channel interacts with its audience. This is also an excellent opportunity to gain content ideas because you will find questions, concerns, or even requests from the community that you can leverage on your channel.

Record as many of the detailed metrics I shared earlier as you can. If you do it manually, then do the best you can. Otherwise, use tools like Social Blade, BuzzSumo, and Tubular Intelligence. Once you've done this extensive research, start looking for the gaps in content and brainstorm how to improve on what you've seen out there. Document every idea, no matter how trivial it may seem. These notes will come in handy as we get into strategy and implementation.

CHAPTER 05

Branding Your Channel

It's time to get to the fun and creative part of setting up your channel. Now that you know what your channel will be about and whom you'll be creating content for, we need to make the different graphics, artwork, and other necessary pieces so that your channel can instantly attract potential subscribers. That's where branding comes in.

Why You Need to Brand

You'll find different definitions of a brand in today's digital world. I want to keep things simple, so here's how we will approach this branding concept.

Branding is about taking your best aspects and recreating them online so that people can have a real sense of who you are and what you stand for the moment they land on your YouTube channel. It's a lot harder to make a great first impression online, so by giving your channel an identity that's true to you, there's a higher chance you'll bridge that gap better and use technology to reinforce relationships rather than hinder them.

Branding has become extremely important on YouTube because you need to stand out and attract the proper attention from the right people. Social media has also become dominated by alluring aesthetics. Like it or not, if your channel doesn't look appealing to the audience you wish to attract, it will be tough to gain momentum. Most importantly, I emphasize branding a lot on YouTube because it is a social platform built around the concept of community at the end of the day and sharing knowledge and ideas. That means there's a strong need for a sense of belonging for the people hanging out there. Your branding does wonders when it comes to creating a signpost with your core identity written all over it, and that helps your "tribe" recognize and connect with you.

How do You go About Establishing Your Brand?

That must be completed on time. It is a natural growth process that will improve as you create content and interact with community members. However, a few key questions will enable us to start the journey of branding your YouTube channel. Ask yourself the following:

- Who am I, and how do I want to be known on YouTube? For example, a speaker, digital marketer, life coach, etc.

- What kind of voice do I want to build on YouTube? For example, funky, laid back, humorous, formal, etc.

- What kind of vocabulary, personality, and verbiage will I use? For example, think of Gary Vee. His language and vocabulary are very distinct. You want to figure out what yours is.

- What emotions, experiences, and benefits do you want your tribe to have from consuming your content?
- What colors and designs will you be using to stand out?

These are just a few questions you must answer as you build your brand. In this chapter, I will walk you through the key elements and how to set each up. Follow along, and your channel will be ready for launch by this end.

Setting Up Your New YouTube Channel

If you already have a channel, you may skip this section if you like, but I still encourage you to go through it. To get started, you must first sign up for a Gmail account. If you already have a Google account, head to youtube.com and click the Sign In button in the top right corner.

If you create the account for the first time, you will be asked to choose whether to make a channel for yourself or a business once you sign up. You will have the option of creating a personal brand or business brand, depending on your objective.

You will need to fill out the details, such as your name the name you want to use for the channel, and then choose to verify the account. Later, you can add a channel manager if you've set up a business channel. To prove your channel, you must give a mobile number where a text or voice message will be sent with a code. Once the code is entered and accepted, YouTube will let you upload videos longer than 15 minutes, add custom thumbnails, do Livestream, and so much more. So please make sure you do this as fast as possible.

Once done, you can head to your channel dashboard and see a blank canvas to add your creativity and personality. This is where the fun begins. If you have other social media profiles or websites you'd like to add to the main dashboard, you can add them here. For now, the most essential step is adding the artwork and graphics to personalize your channel and make it more appealing to your ideal audience.

Channel Images

Let's pick out the main image elements for your channel. Even if you're not a design expert, you can still create incredible images without spending a fortune or hiring expensive graphics designers. Tools such as Canva, PicMonkey, Word Swagg, and Picktochart are just a few of the tools you need to add to your toolbox. These software products are either free or low-cost and require little to no experience in graphics design. My preferred is, of course, Canva, which has a free and pro version. With Canva, you can design epic-looking images in seconds, from your channel art and logo to your thumbnails.

Hire a professional to create your graphics. You can hire a professional to create your channel art with a small budget.

Websites such as 99designs are great for outsourcing, but you can also go to Upwork or Fiverr and hire someone for as little as $5 if you know exactly what you want.

Once you have the main channel image, it's time to brand your new channel. Here's how:

Sign into your YouTube studio, and from the left menu, select Customization. Use the tabs to customize your channel by changing the profile picture, banner image, and video watermark. This is also where you'll have the ability to change the layout.

For the profile picture, YouTube recommends uploading a JPG, GIF, BMP, or PNG file of 800 X 800 px. It can be square or round and renders at 98 X 98 px. Don't use animated GIFs for this.

For the banner image, you need a minimum dimension of 2048 X 1152 px, with an aspect ratio of 16:9. The file size must be 6MB or smaller. If you go with the minimum recommended dimensions, ensure the area for text and logos is 1235 X 338 px. Larger images may get cropped on specific devices because the banner comes across differently depending on whether it is viewed on desktop, mobile, or TV displays.

For basic channel info, you also can personalize what is displayed by adding or removing the information you want to be shared with the public. You must create a brand account if you want a different name from your Google Account. This would be different from your personal Google Account, making it easier to give other people (team members) access to your YouTube channel without sharing your Google Account details. It's also great if you know you'll want to have multiple channels in one account. I highly recommend getting a Brand Account for influencers because of its flexibility. The best part is you can call your channel whatever name you like.

Channel Layout

You can customize your channel so that new viewers and potential subscribers can see your channel trailers, certain featured sections, or a featured video when they first land on your homepage. Channel trailers are great because they offer the new visitor a preview of your channel and what you're all about. It's a great way to make a positive first impression and connect with your audience. Setting up a trailer video is easy. Just select Customization and then "Layout." Once you see "Video spotlight," click ADD and select the video you want to make the trailer. Hit publish, and you'll have your very own trailer. Making a great video trailer is essential, so keep reading to learn how to create an epic video that leaves your audience wanting more.

If you want to avoid having a trailer for the homepage, you could also feature a particular video. Some YouTubers place their most-watched video as the first thing a new visitor sees so they can immediately receive value and see why everyone else has subscribed to that channel. So don't feel pressured to create a trailer; even a high-value content piece will work just as well.

Activity #5: Create Your Channel

Now that you have all the essential elements of setting up your channel, it's time to implement what you've learned. Before you get into the next chapter, decide what kind of channel you want to set up and then get to work coming up with the design, image profile, and logo if necessary. Then, head over to YouTube and create your channel. Feel free to explore the different menus in YouTube Studio and read their community guidelines. Section four of this book will cover more on navigating YouTube Studio, but I want you to start immediately. Create your channel now.

SECTION 03

Creating YouTube Videos

YouTube is a large ecosystem, and although building a solid channel and learning the site is crucial, videos make it tick. Here are detailed YouTube video creation tactics people can't stop discussing.

As every successful YouTuber would tell you, quality beats quantity. But how can we measure quality? Unique ideas or new spins on familiar themes stand out in a sea of information. Your material is more relevant when it meets readers' current needs. Videos that garner comments, likes, and shares do better. Ask questions, survey, and debate.

Different Video Formats.

You can pick from several content types:

- Increase your expertise with lessons and guides.
- Authors share their lives and opinions through vlogs.
- Conversations with influential or topic matter experts.

- Critiques of media, entertainment, and products.
- Real-time spectator interaction during live streams.
- Documentaries are in-depth.

YouTube video streaming/recording: Make sure everything is in order before recording. The primary gear is better to start with. For beginners, a smartphone usually works. Later, you can improve your camera, microphone, and lighting. Keep the space peaceful and well-lit. Consider the setting—it must be unaffected. Even if you don't memorize lines, a good script will keep your video on track.

Editing makes content more engaging and polished. Cut, trim, and splice film to learn video editing. Remove errors and unnecessary material. These assist viewers in keeping on track as the video switches scenes or topics. Transitions and visuals: Exercise caution. Title animation, remarks, and relevant graphics are essential, but overuse can distract.

Speak clearly. The background music should match the subject, but it should keep your speech intact.

Regular uploads show subscribers your reliability. How often do you post, but what, how, and how well? Schedule uploads weekly, bimonthly, or monthly you may manage. Brand your videos using recognizable opening and closing sequences, imagery, and color schemes.

Avoid abrupt changes in tone or presentation.

Teamwork expands your channel's reach. Find content providers with similar audiences—collaborations featuring guest appearances on each channel. Working collaboratively on a project lets both authors use their expertise.

YouTube videos demand creativity, technical expertise, and brand cohesion. Know your audience, provide them value, and improve. Remember that each video we view will teach you something new. Feedback, analytics, and trends will guide improvements. However, your narrative is crucial. If you deliver well, people will listen.

CHAPTER 06

Creating Quality Content

This section of our book focuses on creating fantastic content to get you views and subscribers. For creatives, this is the most exciting part of their YouTube channel management. But why invest time in learning how to create quality content?

- Your content will stand out more if the quality is better than your competitors.
- Quality content is usually so packed with value that a new audience can't help but want more of what you're creating, which will lead to more subscribers.
- With great content comes the potential of going viral.
- Quality content will serve you for years to come.

We call it evergreen content only because once you create it, the number of views, engagement, and potential business grows over time. I have a video that's three years old and still brings in new business inquiries.

What Exactly Is Quality Content?

As stated, quality refers to the experience of the user. You can have lots of bells and whistles on your video, but if the users have a poor experience, then it won't matter. That content will be considered a flop. Quality includes all the technical aspects of video, including audio quality, visual quality, editing quality, and the quality of the shared script or content. For example, consider whether the video will be HD or 4K. Then, ask yourself, are the colors right? Is the lighting proper? Is it sharp and crisp? Is the audio good? Was it edited in a way that makes sense and tells a story? These are a few examples of objective quality, and the best part is that they are measurable and easy to control on your part.

However, we also need to think about subjective quality. We care about these as human beings, which will directly influence your channels' growth. It includes making it relevant, interesting, and engaging to the end-user.

According to a Google report, "when people choose what to watch, relating to their passions is 1.6X more important than whether the content has high production quality." I'm sharing this to inform you that objective and subjective quality matter. And while the objective is easy to measure and control, the emotional quality will ultimately determine how well your channel does in the long run.

We want to ensure you have the best chance of winning the

hearts and attention of your potential subscribers. The best way to do that is to combine the technical aspects of video production with world-class content that resonates with the targeted audience. It would be best if you come across as relatable, and the stuff you put out should be focused on providing value in some way, shape, or form—more on how to do that in the unfolding chapters.

The Different Kinds of Video Content

Growing your YouTube channel can be manageable and straightforward. You need to know which types of content people love to watch and create more of those types. Here are the top ones.

- How-to and Tutorials
- Behind-the-scenes video content.
- Interview and Q&A
- Pranks
- Vlog
- Product reviews
- 360
- User-generated content
- Webinar

- Presentation
- Livestream

• How-to and Tutorials

Most famous YouTubers you might know have gotten that rise to stardom through this content category. Millennials are exceptional at creating this type of video content. It performs well because people love watching videos, and they love watching actionable insights. Some YouTubers have gone from zero to earning over $50 million by creating excellent tutorials.

I love this type of content because you're not limited by anything, and you can be as creative as you want. You can't go wrong if you understand your audience's values and create lots and lots of free content around it. It can be tutorials on anything under the sun. This is the age of information, and people love to learn. Ensure the tutorials are high quality to help, not make a sale!

• Behind-the-scenes video content

These types of videos are great for companies and solopreneurs. They are firmly rooted in raw storytelling for branding purposes. What do I mean by that? It's about revealing what you stand for and the culture you're building as a team or organization, and it pulls back the curtain on your brand to allow customers and potential buyers to forge a connection with it. It goes from being an impersonal operation to actual human beings with emotions, frustrations, ambitions, and personalities. If you have a remote team, get creative about how to record and edit funny behind-the-scenes content. If you fly solo, you can show a behind-the-scenes or sneak peek video about an upcoming project. A great example of this type of content can be found on Mind Valley Academy or Vistaprint.

- **Interview and Q&A**

These types of video content are great for authority building. Suppose you can get influences, experts, or even celebrities to come and answer your questions. In that case, you'll start attracting the attention of those who resonate with that information. This video content lets you connect with and align your brand with inspiring people and thought leaders. It also helps you look more trustworthy since you're hanging out with and getting answers from a respected voice.

A good interview requires planning, but don't make it appear too polished and scripted. It should be natural and intimate so potential subscribers can fully immerse themselves in that experience and feel like they know you and your guest better. As the interviewer, you need to ask powerful questions, direct the interview in the best direction, and make it as meaningful as possible for the user. I love interviews because you can create lots of evergreen content without running out of ideas or topics. You can even give exclusive access to your audience by tapping into well-known influencers and celebrities. There's a lot of power in leveraging this if you know how to do it right. A great example is Lewis Howes's "School of Greatness."

• Pranks

A huge and hungry audience awaits you on YouTube if you enjoy pulling off pranks. These types of video content are primarily for entertainment. As the creator, you would prank a friend or stranger and capture it on film. Of course, you must ensure the pranks are subtle enough to avoid offending anyone. What you're looking for is to make people laugh and disrupt their day or their thought patterns. Some people have been extreme and created a lot of controversies, and it has worked. Still, I strongly urge you to avoid that because, based on what I've seen, people enjoy funny pranks, not offensive or extreme pranks.

• Vlog

These are video blogs. They are usually raw and require minimal cost production. All you need is a unique brand voice and a personality that resonates with your target audience. Most vlogs are off-the-cuff and unpolished. All you need is a smartphone or webcam as equipment. I encourage you to have a script or bullet point to ensure your content is concise and well-thought-out. As a video influencer, you could do daily vlogs sharing your day at work. Think of this as documenting your journey. Share whatever you're in the trenches trying to build with the community, and you'll start to see a tribe joining you on the ride. I suggest checking out Gary Vaynerchuck's "Daily Vee" for inspiration on this type of video content.

• Product Reviews

This type of video content is like how-to content. It's meant to be insightful and focused on helping, not selling a product. Consumers flock to YouTube every minute of the hour, looking for help along their purchase journey. They want to know which product is best, how it works, and whether it will be good value for their money. A product review can help answer all those questions. However, I recommend doing product reviews once you've established credibility and trust with your audience because they need to trust you before following your advice—affiliate marketing partners up very well with product review videos. But again, you will need to walk that fine line of helping your audience make the right decision, not just selling them something because you're making money. By the way, you don't need to talk about products in your niche. For example, if you're a personal trainer, you could talk about the best running shoes or home workout equipment - even if they aren't directly related to you. Bringing that service and customer-focused value to an audience can cause someone to trust you and even hire your personal training services. Think creatively about which products you review and intend to bring value.

• 360 or VR content

360-degree videos are our latest alternatives as we move closer to a complete virtual experience. Yes, we still have a long way to go, but people dig 360 content as it is immersive and puts the users in the center of the action, allowing them to pan around the room with their smart device. In other words, this type of content focuses more on bringing the end-user an immersive and exciting experience. Don't think you need to be fancy or have a huge company to make these videos work for you. Experiment and see if it matches your brand and personality.

• **User-generated content**

This type of video content will work once you have a growing customer base. If you have a business, find creative ways to get previous or existing customers to create social content. Something sharable that sells for you. User-generated content has become massive on social media. It's a great way to get free testimonials, demonstrate your credibility, and gather new leads because people love to see social proof. Most social media users say that UGC is the most authentic type of content, and they want to see more of it. So whether you're just starting and need time to build a customer list or already have people who can create this for you, come up with a plan and incentive to make people want to record short videos about how great your brand is—wondering how to get started? Consider running a contest on YouTube and other social media platforms. Encourage people to send over videos of themselves using your product. Or you can start a campaign for your brand and products and create a trending hashtag, then ask people to use it as much as possible.

• Webinar

Did you know you could host webinars on Google Hangout? It's simple and easy to navigate. This type of video content is precious for an audience that loves to learn. It can exponentially grow your YouTube channel because you can offer and share webinars on your channel. Just make sure it's educative and actionable information. Since the pandemic in 2020, we've seen a massive spike in virtual webinars, so now people are accustomed to learning online. If you don't want to use Google Hangouts, you can do Zoom webinars and then upload the recording to your YouTube channel. Think of webinars as a free live event. This is an opportunity for your potential subscribers to learn something valuable from you and begin the purchase journey. It can be a solo webinar or a roundtable panel discussion with several gurus in your niche.

• Presentations

Have you ever heard of Ted Talks? Of course you have! These are a form of presentation content; as you know, they perform well on YouTube. A presentation type of video content (even if it's not a Ted Talk) can work well because it combines the excitement of a live event with a virtual webinar's practicality to create something compelling and shareable. You could be on the other side of the planet watching a presentation from someone you could have never met. Of course, if you want to do Ted Talks, you can do that too, but there's a long process of making that happen. If you will leverage this video content, please start by giving as many presentations as possible at different locations. The size of the audience doesn't matter. Ensure the presentation is excellent, and you capture the whole thing on video.

• **Livestreaming**

The last type of video content we will discuss is Live streaming, which was added a few years ago. Since then, there has been increasing demand across all social platforms, including YouTube. People love interacting in a Livestream, and it is expected to become a $70.5 billion industry by 2021. YouTube allows you to participate and enjoy a portion of that success. The best part about live streaming is that you can do it in any category, niche, and subject matter. Places such as cooking, self-improvement, motivational speeches, DIY arts and crafts, makeup routines, dance choreography, workout routines, yoga, meditation, etc. can all perform great on the Live stream.

Why does this work so well? It comes down to the fact that people love the suspense of Live video. They can't resist the urge to tune in because they don't want to miss out on getting new gossip, learning something new, or connecting with someone they admire.

Studies have shown that live streams generate up to 10 times more engagement than regular videos. Neil Patel said that live video broadcasts receive 600% more engagement than regular posts. So what are you waiting for?

You can be completely unknown today, but if you create great content, you can become a YouTube superstar using any content type in no time.

Why You Need a Solid Video Content Strategy

Creating a well-thought-out video content strategy is necessary if you want long-term success. Here's the thing. Building brand authority or a robust library that keeps drawing in traffic will take time. That's okay. Instead of fussing about the daunting work ahead of you, focus on creating a simple and easy-to-execute system you can follow. Ensure your plan is flexible because you'll need to adjust as you grow.

Why do you need to come up with a clear strategy? Because if you don't, you'll end up disheartened and feeling like you're not progressing. That will likely cause you to give up too soon. It will also be hard to measure and monitor your growth if everything is random. Posting a content idea that comes to you occasionally will not bring you the change you need. Trust me on that. And more importantly, I want to help ensure you always stay focused on content ideas. The more precise and well-planned your strategy, the easier it is to keep producing even after a dry spell.

So, how do we go about creating your strategy? I borrowed insights from Think with Google, who share many relevant ideas on winning big on YouTube. They interview and run case studies on some of the biggest brands in the world. Think

Johnson & Johnson, Nike, and even Marvel Movies. It's only wise to listen to their advice on building fantastic content on our YouTube channels. We may need more resources or money to create at the level of these giant corporations. Still, we can implement the same principles driving their success. A simple framework I have learned from studying those case studies is to Create, Collaborate, and curate.

The 3 C's for A Simple And Efficient Content Strategy

Create

Your strategy should include a detailed brainstorm of the titles, keywords, lessons, or subject matter your videos will cover over a certain period. We can call this a video content plan. For this section of your strategy, you will need to research the top-performing content in your niche market and then make a list of what you will create.

Depending on your preference, you can have a monthly or 90-day content plan. I recommend starting with a 30-day content plan to stay calm. Then, decide whether you'll batch these videos together so you can shoot once or twice a week. If you're bold and committed to being on camera a lot, you can also shoot, edit, and publish on the same day. I recommend giving yourself enough leeway for emergencies, equipment glitches, and editing time.

If you plan to release one new video daily, the above options work well. If you remove more than one video daily, you must batch your video recordings to allow ample editing and personalization time. Remember, the quantity must not compromise the quality of your video content.

Collaborate

Creating strategic partnerships is the best way to build up your library and grow your brand on YouTube. A section on your content strategy should exist for collaborations with peers and other YouTube influencers. The great benefit of partnering up with others in your space is your channel's increased exposure.

Make sure, however, that the agreement is mutually beneficial. I recommend creating an outreach campaign once you've hit your first 1K subscribers. And when you do, begin with those most likely to agree to this partnership. For example, asking someone with 3 million subscribers to collaborate when you only have 1K followers may yield negative results. You need to pay them handsomely to ensure these categories of YouTubers are out of reach at first. But if you started reaching out to influencers with 5K - 30K subscribers, they will likely want to work with you if you can prove how valuable the experience will be.

When you collaborate, you co-create the video content and then cross-post on each other's channels for maximum exposure. Not only will you be adding to your library, but you'll also bring value to a new audience that didn't know you existed.

For example, there's a YouTuber with a channel on physics experiments and how to apply them to everyday life. She collaborated with a guy with a channel for testing and reviewing tech gear. Their collaboration involved using physics to see whether the iPhone 11 Pro could withstand a massive hit without breaking. The video was entertaining and cool to watch, plus we learned a lot about Vacuum and how powerful nature is. Even the iPhone isn't built to withstand the powers of Mother Nature. I share this simple example to show you what's possible with collaborations. You can find the video on both channels and now, the tech-savvy geeks who didn't know about the physics channel got a chance to subscribe and follow "Physics Girl." That's the power of a good collaboration.

Curate

The last C we want to add to your content strategy involves curating content. This isn't content you create. Instead, it comes from existing customers, subscribers, and loyal fans who want to praise you and your brand. That's why this part of your content comes when the channels begin to mature because it's likely you're starting from scratch, and that's okay. Just know that you can do this type of content at some point, and it'll boost your credibility and authority. Fans and customers love sharing their experiences, stories, and opinions. Getting this type of content will be easy, especially if you're regularly running contests and giveaways. Think of it to invite your audience to help you tell your story on YouTube.

A content strategy doesn't need to be perfect, but you must have one. With these three different areas, you also want to know what metrics and measurements of growth you'll be going after. As a beginner, here's a simple template I encourage you to follow.

- Write down the big and little goals that lead up to that big one.
- Write down who the content is for.
- Write down the influencers your audience follows on YouTube.
- Please write down the experience you want the audience to have and how the content should impact them.
- Write down your expected milestones and principal return on investment (ROI).

How To Plan with Your Content

The more thought you put into your video content before hitting that record button, the better the quality and performance. Whether you're doing a technical how-to or a daily vlog, it's essential to plan. How much planning you do is entirely up to you. Some people want to script out every word. Others need a vague idea of the main message they want to pass on before shooting. There's no wrong or right here. Your personality and experience with being on camera influence how you plan your video content. Still, I will share a few best practices below.

Remember that the first place to start, as stated earlier, is with a documented content plan. It can be two weeks, thirty days, sixty days, or even a ninety-day plan. If you're one of those who cannot start thinking too far ahead, then opt for a weekly program. Sit with your journal or a Google document and plan the video content topic, title, and key points you'll create over the specified period. You can also use a content calendar for this. If you approach your content planning from the perspective of creating a viral video or a single piece of content that will make you an overnight sensation, then you will fail. Those short-term rewards have nothing to do with growing your channel or brand. Instead, focus on creating consistent content that will engage your audience. The sweet spot to hit is that point of intersection between what your brand stands for and what your audience cares about.

Researching content topics

If you have an existing customer base or a following on another social media platform, you can create a questionnaire asking your current fans what they'd love to learn from you. Social media users are very interested in sharing opinions and offering suggestions. If you don't have any followers, look at your competitors and peers. Subscribe to their channel on YouTube to see what's working and where the gaps are. Please read all the comments on their most engaged posts. These are all great places to get new title ideas and topics.

Once the research is done, it's time to get specific and decide on the types of keywords you'll focus on. You'll need more informational keywords if your channel is more educational and informative. But if the content focuses on selling, you'll need more transactional keywords integrated into your video content, title, descriptions, and tags.

A content plan should be integrated with your calendar using software like Asana, Buffer, etc. You can also create your own using a spreadsheet. All you need to have in the columns is the publish date, title/description, status (in progress, completed, delayed), type of content, and main keywords.

How To Structure the Video Content - A Simple Template

- Map out the first 15 seconds.
- Outline the key points.
- Use the proven formula H.I.C.C (Hook Intro Content Call-to-action)

Hook

The hook is the thing that will grab attention and get people to watch the video. Include it at the beginning of your video within that 15-second window so people don't click away.

Intro

The intro helps the audience understand what you'll cover, why they should listen to you or care, and a bit about yourself as the host.

Content

This is the meat of your video. All the value goes into this section, and it should take up the most time because you will be giving people what you promised at the beginning of the video. For example, if you're a personal trainer, this part would be the workout to tighten your abs.

Call-to-action

Always have a call to action at the end of each video. Summarize what the video was about, especially if it was informational or educational, and then ask them to act. Even if it was purely an entertainment video, you could still add a call to action by asking your audience to subscribe, like, share, or comment on the video.

Keep your video structure super simple by following the above form until you get the hang of things. Then you can get a bit fancier.

Collaborating With Other Creators in Your Niche

As I said before, a strong content strategy always has a section for collaborations. The smart YouTubers understand the importance of leveraging this tactic. Still, you should know there are some advantages and disadvantages to using this method.

Pros:

- Collaborations are free, so it's a great way to tap into an existing audience without spending money.

- It exposes you to a new audience, benefiting a young channel.

- It enables you to create more content.

- The quality of content improves because you always learn so much from these types of partnerships, especially if done with someone who has been around a lot longer than you.

- It's a powerful way to establish connections and build genuine relationships with people who share your passion and desire to serve an audience. Some of these collaborations may turn into new lucrative opportunities.

Cons:

While I don't believe in disadvantages when creating collaboration because every experience has something to teach us (even those that don't work out), I can share a few things to become aware of.

- It will require a lot of upfront energy to get these relationships started. You are 100% responsible for getting their attention and making them interested in your offer.

- It would be best if you did many follow-ups when going

after your list of potential collaborators.

- You might experience lots of rejection, and that's okay. Learn to handle these situations.

When doing collaborations, make sure you give and serve first. Don't be overly self-promotional. Most importantly, be authentic. If you are fully confirmed, you will only resonate with a new audience and have them interested in checking out your channel, so don't try to "fake it" or "fit in." This will ensure you get the most out of that experience.

I also encourage you to go into it open-minded and focused on having fun. It doesn't matter how many people end up subscribing. Learn to take your mind off metrics and data and be a passionate creator. That will make the influencer you're working with also appreciate the experience, as they will see you care more about serving the audience than getting subscribers, which might lead to more collaborative opportunities.

How To Make Sure You Never Run Out of Great Ideas

You'll hear many content creators talk about going through a "dry spell," and at some point, you might find yourself experiencing the same. So, let's talk about how to handle these situations. The worst thing to do is force yourself to get on camera when you feel completely drained of value and inspiration.

I usually encourage clients to take a day or a week away from the spotlight and reset. Sometimes, the pressure becomes too much and causes our creative juices to stagnate. However, my advice only works if you already have enough content in the pipeline to allow you that "off-time." I encourage you to batch your content creation and schedule it beforehand. At a minimum, one week early. Some people prefer to design it a month in advance. Whichever frequency you choose, ensure you have enough ready-to-go content so you're not rushing or banging your head against the wall because it's Monday morning, and you have nothing to post. To help ensure you have enough ideas, here are some best practices.

- Once a week, sit with a Google doc and write down all the titles you want to create content for.

- Always carry a pen and notepad or train your Siri to be alert when ideas come to you while running errands, working out, driving, etc. Some of the best ideas come to us when we least expect them.

- Download an app such as Evernote to help you capture screenshots, save, and bookmark links that inspire you as you browse the Internet.

You might come across an article or video that stirs up your creative juices, and there's nothing worse than trying to find that link (days later) in your long browser history.

A Simple Formula to Get Over 100 Video Content Ideas in Less Than 20min.

• Content Topic Generators

These are your most accessible source of inspiration and content ideas. You could have content for a month in less than twenty minutes. The list of content generators continues to grow, so keep checking for new ones. How it works is that these software apps use the most popular title formulas and fill in the blanks with your specific terms and keywords. Check out

1. Portent Content Idea Generator
2. ContentIdeator
3. Content Strategy Helper
4. Hubspot's Topic Generator

• Buzzsumo

Head over to Buzzsumo and type in the keyword you want to discuss. You'll see a breakdown of all the most famous content based on social shares. It's a great way to know what people love, and when you find articles that are doing well, a video version will likely perform well. With their free version, you're limited to a few searches, but it should be enough to get your juices flowing, and you can see what's done well in the recent weeks, months, even a year ago.

• **Ubersuggest**

This tool gives you a lot more than content ideas. It also shares keyword ideas and tells you which content is doing well based on search volume. It's a great way to see the top-ranking sites and the range, making them rank so high that you can leverage those titles.

• **Answer The Public**

This tool helps you find all the common questions about the keyword you type in. In just a few seconds, you can have abundant content ideas and similar keywords organized in an easy-to-read diagram that you can easily download. The tool offers keyword alternatives like comparisons, prepositions, and related phrases.

• **Quora**

Quora is a trendy Q&A platform that has gained much traction recently. Head to the forum and type in the keywords or topics you want to be an authority on. Then, look at all the questions asked in your niche and pick the ones people are most interested in. You can tell by the number of followers and the number of upvotes for the top responses.

Once you find a hot question, shoot a video with your best answer. Be as educational, informative, and helpful as possible in that video. Try to be comprehensive with your reply so that when people click to watch the video, they can immediately see the value you bring and hopefully subscribe. But you still need to finish.

Once you've published the video, return to Quora's original question. Answer it with a few words explaining your thoughts and letting people know you've shot a video with a more detailed answer. You can link the video here to drive traffic directly to your YouTube video. I recommend keeping a spreadsheet with the list of questions and a direct link so it's easy to find them again once you've shot the video. It also helps you track performance because you can check once a month to see if people responded and voted you up. It's impossible with Quora to run out of ideas because you don't need to come up with any. Just find questions you can best answer on video.

Aside from Quora and Answer the Public, you can also check forums like Yahoo, Reddit, or specific industry forums where your audience most likely hangs out. You want to find questions, problems, complaints, or inquiries that people bounce back and forth in these forums.

- **Online Groups**

These include Facebook groups, LinkedIn, Twitter Chats, Instagram Pods, etc. People get together to discuss interesting topics or even complain about products or services that might belong to your competitors. Look for groups that only allow a few articles to be shared to avoid spammy ones. The best groups or pods have lots of questions and answers.

• Industry Publications and Blog Comment Sections

Most people must realize what a goldmine it can be to spend half an hour going through your favorite publication's comment section. Suppose you're a personal trainer or dietician wanting to create unique content. By browsing big online blogs such as Bulletproof and other health publications, you will likely come across many great ideas from their readers. Sometimes, readers will even ask questions or raise concerns over something that needs to be covered. Those are the gaps your video content should fill. The demand is there, and your content can be the solution.

• YouTubers You Follow

I already asked you in an earlier chapter to list your top competitors. These are the people who are already crushing it in your niche. You need to be subscribed to their channels to learn and get inspired by them. One of your competitors created content six months ago that's now a little dated, or they may only share a brief overview of the topic. Still, you can go deeper and create something even better. That's your ticket to growth and value-adding.

• Social Media Influencers You Follow

With this hack, you want to research all your top social media profiles to see whom you follow or who follows you and shares great content. Look at what they engage with and see if there are any topics you can add to your content planner.

• Webinars

Most people don't think about this when first getting started, but given how popular webinars have become, it's a great place to get content ideas. Check out popular websites in your niche. Research the top influencers in your industry who usually do webinars and follow them to see topics they keep running webinars on. The most popular webinar titles would also be great for video content.

• HARO (Help A Reporter Out)

Helping a reporter out is a great place to see trending topics, and it can be an opportunity for your brand to be featured. When you share your expertise on the platform, a reporter can pick up your story and share it with the world, giving you free publicity. But I am sharing this platform with you because by being on it, you get a glimpse of what people are looking for in terms of topics and stories.

• Google

If your keywords are correct, Google can show you trends (go to Google Trends) or related searches from the search bar. By clicking on the tabs labeled "Video," you can also see the top-ranking videos in your niche, indicating what area to focus on. Google also added a section called "People also ask," - which is great for finding more questions about your topic or keyword. All these are great spots for coming up with fresh and relevant content.

• **Self-help magazines**

There's a reason why magazines like Men's Health and Cosmo are so popular. These magazines tend to have highly clickable titles. They know how to give people what they want. I have a friend who first opened my eyes to this little trick. Now I use it all the time. Whenever I am in a store, I look for the magazine section to browse some of these popular magazines quickly. You can do the same. Just take a quick snapshot of the titles most resonating with you and add your industry's words.

• **Amazon**

Amazon is another excellent hack because it is an endless ocean of content. You can create many "how-to" content or answer questions left in the comment section of books, apparel, or whatever else your niche focuses on. Since there's a book written on almost every topic under the sun, consider browsing authors in your industry and look for bestsellers. Then, open to read the table of contents for title ideas. If you want to hit a vein of gold, go through the comments people leave and compile them into more content ideas. Although this might take a little longer than twenty minutes, it'll be worth your time, and you will end up with ideas that last a year.

Do You Need a Script? Yes Or No?

While it would be easier to give a yes or no answer... the honest answer is - it depends. As the content creator, you can determine what's wrong or suitable for you. This scenario has no one-size-fits-all because some people swear by script writing and teleprompters. In contrast, others would rather die than script out their content. You can start with either and see which fits best. Still, suppose you're a complete newbie. In that case, I encourage you to practice scripting or, at the very least, create bullet points and prompters to assist you as you build confidence in front of the camera.

If you already know scriptwriting is not for you because you've tried it for a while and it didn't pan out, no matter what you did, please skip over to the activity section of this chapter. But a script will be the best way to go if you're unsure and feel your confidence still needs to be improved. It can be as simple as having a bullet point on a sheet of paper dangling next to your camera, where you can easily read the main points. Or get a teleprompter and write out a killer video script. Remember, this isn't a movie screenplay. You're creating something for a social network, so the flow of it will have to be different. Here is a guideline to follow:

Get the Essential Elements Right.

As we said before, you have a fifteen-second window on YouTube to grab the attention of your potential subscribers. If you miss that window, the user will likely click away, and we don't want that. So, prioritize the hook and flow of the content.

Create a basic model for your script that can be explained in 1min. Break down the main points so you can easily communicate your message without losing the viewer. People need to understand your concept quickly.

Make sure the audio is of excellent quality. Audio matters a lot! If you add background music, ensure it doesn't overpower or disrupt your voice. Don't you hate it when you can't hear what the guy says in his cooking video because of the loud music? Don't do that to your audience.

Have a strong point of view.

Your YouTube channel is supposed to show what your brand stands for. Having a clear point of view and confidently expressing it is essential. People who struggle to share their opinions boldly rarely do well on this platform. Since we've gone through exercises in earlier chapters to determine your channel's identity and your target audience, be sure to speak your opinion authentically and confidently about the topic you cover.

Pacing.

When writing out the script, be sure to pace yourself accordingly. Add only a few filler words or create awkward silence in your content. Let it flow naturally like you're sitting with a friend in Starbucks having coffee. And please don't be like those late-night infomercials guys who barely breathe between sentences. Take your time to meet a specific deadline. Pace yourself and keep a steady tempo that is true to your personality.

Include lots of emotional words and triggers.

Do you know why a video prank of a teenage daughter scaring her mom performs better than a reporter talking about inflation? Simple. Emotional content will always get more views because people can relate to it more.

Be clear, concise, and conversational.

Whether you create a detailed script or an outline, it's crucial to be conversational and concise. To help ensure you do this, I suggest you avoid writing lengthy sentences when writing. Videos don't require too many words because onscreen visuals accompany them, so you don't have to worry about using significant, complex sentences. If anything, stick to terminology and penalties that a 6th grader can easily follow.

Example template to follow:

Introduction. The first fifteen seconds of your video make or break your chances of winning a potential subscriber, so make your introduction short, sweet, and attention-grabbing. Introduce yourself and the topic at the beginning of the script, and please remember to add a strong hook.

When scripting this part, ensure the first few lines contain the hook to keep people tuned. Follow it up with a clear breakdown of what the audience will learn by the end of the video. Example: Are you freaking out because it's just a few weeks to your wedding day, and you still haven't shed those extra pounds for your big day? Fear not, because, by the end of this video, you'll know precisely how to drop at least ten pounds in the next five days without ever hitting the gym! I'm Jenny, and for the past fifteen years, I've been helping couples look hot for their big day and that special honeymoon week. Let's get you lean and ready to enjoy your special day now!

Main Content and Ask an engaging question.

Once the intro is done, script out the main content. This is the meat of the video. I often like to include questions to keep the viewer's attention. Something simple that gives a yes or no answer should do it, and it's a great way to encourage people to comment. In this section, script out word for word what you're going to teach. Returning to the example I just shared, scripting this section would require Jenny to write exactly how the viewer will shed those ten pounds within five days. What are the steps? What secret hacks or ingredients should the viewer know about?

That is also where a story would come in handy. Suppose Jenny has experienced this process of transformation. In that case, she can talk about how she did it and shed that weight before her special day. Perhaps one of her clients has an incredible transformation story that could be interjected here with a few before and after snapshots. Storytelling will keep the viewer glued to the screen and give them a glimpse of how powerful this solution is.

When scripting your content, be conversational, don't use big words, and make it short and punchy. The more concise you are, the easier it will be to edit the video and the more engaging it will be for the viewer.

Summary and call to action

In this last part, as you bring the video to an end, I suggest you do a quick recap of all the good stuff they learned. That is especially important if you're teaching something. Otherwise, summarise the main idea and tie it back to your main objective if there's a specific action step like downloading something, signing up for an event or program, etc. When you have softer CTAs, you can sprinkle them throughout the video, such as "Before we jump into the main secrets I want to share, let me remind you to hit the subscribe button so you never miss another cool video like this one." Ultimately, you can also say, "If you liked this video, give it a thumbs up and share it with a friend."

Activity #6: Create And Schedule Your Content

Now that you've learned how to plan your content and where to find great ideas, it's time for action. Create a list of the video titles you will shoot over the next 90 days. Get your content calendar out and start brainstorming and researching using the various hacks you learned in this chapter. By the end of this exercise (before starting the next chapter), you should have ninety potential video titles mapped out on your content planner. Schedule a time to create, edit, and publish each content on a calendar. Don't worry if you just got a panic attack when I mentioned video editing. Yes, it can be a daunting process, but the next chapter two chapters are designed to ensure you have an easy and fun time. Let's put some ideas on our planner and prep ourselves for success.

Pro Tip:

If you want to stay focused and on-point with your content planning, fill out this simple statement and let it direct your focus on content ideas. Keep this statement in mind, print it, and stick it where you can see it often so you always stay relevant and interesting to your ideal audience.

Complete the following:

The video content I produce helps my brand accomplish …….[name goal]…...and ....[name goal]…... by providing …....[adjective]……. and …….[adjective]……. content that makes…....[name emotion]…... feel...me emotion]…... or...[name benefit]…...so that they can…... [Name benefit]…...

CHAPTER 07

Recording YouTube Videos

Recording your video should be as easy as switching on the camera and pressing the red button. Well, that's true, but a lot more goes into recording. Lots of things must be prepped beforehand. It's known as the pre-recording phase. Many items must also occur once you're done recording (the post-production phase). The pre- and post-recording stages affect the video's overall result, so take advantage of this and the upcoming chapters. This chapter will focus on what you need to know and do to be camera-ready and produce amazing videos. So, before you hit that record button, let's cover some best practices and the type of equipment you'll need to make your YouTube channel successful.

The Only Equipment You Need to Get Started

Video production can be costly; I won't lie. Some YouTubers have invested tens of thousands in having the recording studios, equipment, and crew you see on their channels. I created this book with the simple intention of helping the beginner who may or may not have a budget available yet still wants to create something beautiful. If that's you, this chapter will ease some of your concerns. Whether you can afford to spend a few thousand, hundreds, or zero dollars on equipment, I'm here to show you how to be camera-ready. The essential gear you need includes:

- A camera that can shoot in HD
- Good lighting
- Great Audio
- Video editing software
- Camera stabilizer or mounter

Whether you're broke or have some money to invest, these five things are fundamental to recording your video. I will break down some options for those serious about getting the right equipment, but there are some simple workarounds even if you still need to afford a dime.

Need More Money to Spend? Read This.

If you have no money to invest in equipment, consider using your smartphone camera or the webcam from your laptop. Most of the smartphones come with incredible video quality. The minimum quality standard you need to go for with a camera should be 1080p. Ensure you also have a laptop with free editing software like iMovie (for Mac users).

Of course, you will need to mount the recording gear somewhere, so get creative. If you can't afford a stabilizer like a tripod, stack some books or boxes on a desk near a window to get that natural lighting. You can always use the phone or laptop's built-in audio system when it comes to the audio.

This is going to produce something other than top-notch quality. However, you can still shoot decent videos if you play around with an excellent background and use editing and filters. For free graphics editing, you can use Canva, which is perfect for producing attention-grabbing thumbnails.

Got Some Money to Invest? Read This.

Here are eight (8) essential things to consider if you can invest money into your equipment setup.

The Camera.

Get a camera that shoots in 4K. Since it will be the most critical piece of equipment, please invest to the best of your ability. If you have no limitations with your budget, then the sky is the limit. Your options are plenty. Quality camcorders or webcams (if you're using a laptop to shoot) are great for beginners. Still, if you can afford to spend more, I suggest you buy a DSLR camera. How do you decide what to purchase? Think about your budget and the type of content you'll be creating.

Camcorders are designed to record videos. Hence, they are the easiest to operate, light to carry around, and can handle almost any shooting scenario, whether vlogging on the go or in your basement studio. A good recommendation for this would be the Sony HDRCX405, which costs about $198. What's great about it aside from the pocket-friendly price is that it is full HD with an image stabilization feature, which reduces shaking and blurring when shooting handheld. It can shoot 1080p videos at 60fps and is equipped with a Carl Zeiss zoom lens with 27x true optical zoom for lossless magnification and excellent overall video quality. It also allows you to record in MP4, which makes web uploads super-fast and convenient.

I recommend the Logitech C920 HD Pro for webcams, which goes for about $89.99 and shoots full HD 1080p and 720p. If you're a gamer, this will be a perfect fit because the camcorder uses its processor to encode videos instead of relying greatly on your computer power. That means it won't slow down your computer, which is excellent.

DSLRs are the most favored and highly recommended cameras for YouTubers across all niches. I use that, too, and I'm happy with the quality. I love these cameras because of their adaptability in low-light situations and the polished video recording quality they provide. But trust me, this is for someone willing to invest more money. There are many great options, whether you prefer Sony or Canon, but I will share my two favorite options: Canon Cameras. The first is the Canon 70D, and the second is the Canon EOS Rebel T5i. Both are amazing, so do your research, and based on your budget and content needs, pick one.

The Microphone

There's no way around this. You must invest in a lapel or an omnichannel microphone for excellent audio. Great audio only happens sometimes. Even the best cameras need a little help regarding audio quality.

The microphone you choose can be cheap. You can get a Lavalier mic, which picks up less background noise and is pocket-friendly. You can do something decent starting from as little as $30 on Amazon. If you want to invest a little more, here are some great options.

Get a USB microphone. These mics have become popular with YouTubers because of their ease of use and sound quality. They are also affordable. If you want to go this route, consider getting the Logitech Clear Chat H390 for around $39.99. It's super easy to use and provides a clear, crisp sound. You could also go for Audio-Technica AT2020USB Plus, which costs $149. What's great about this is that it allows self-monitoring through its built-in headphone jack with volume control. It offers mix control so you can blend your microphone with pre-recorded audio.

Go for shotgun microphones if you're serious about becoming a heavy hitter. You'll need to have deeper pockets for these types of microphones. They work great with a small professional camera and have shock mounts that help reduce the noise coming from mechanical vibrations around the mic. These microphones are known for capturing crisp sounds and vocals, even if you're recording outdoors. If your pocket allows, I recommend going for Rode Microphones VideoMic Pro R, which sells for about $299. It's a handy version that's perfect for your DSLR or camcorder. It has a super-cardioid polar pattern system and is powered by 9V batteries, so you can use it for up to 70 hours.

The last option I want to give you is a lavalier mic, aka lapel mic, which is the easiest route. All you need to do is discretely clip it onto your clothes or belt. It comes in a set with a transmitter to which the lapel and receiver connect, allowing sound to be picked up even from great distances. If you're a speaker, you've seen these at conferences. I recommend the RODELink Digital Wireless System, which costs $399, so you'll need a big budget. The benefits make it worthwhile because it works even from a hundred meters away and offers the ability to select the best signal to deliver audio as reliable as cable connections.

Lighting

Natural sunlight is, of course, one of the best lights you can have for your video. Still, you're not at a loss if nature isn't working in your favor as you begin this journey of YouTube stardom. If you can invest in good lighting, even a tiny space in the basement can produce a high-quality video. Lighting greatly influences your setup's mood and brightness, so here are some options to ensure you look professional.

The first recommendation is getting a softbox. It can emulate the natural soft lighting from a window. If you want to go with something subtle, this would be the ideal choice, and the best part is the Flashpoint SoftBox goes for only $49.95. It comes with a 70W fluorescent light unit and an AC plug that's easy to use. You can use this kit indoors with camcorders and digital cameras.

The second recommendation is a ring light. Ring lights are super popular with vloggers. When its ring shape emits light around you, it eliminates shadows from every direction, making you look more attractive in front of the camera. So next time you see those doll-like beauty vloggers - don't envy them; appreciate their creativity and lighting system! If you'd like a similar setup, experiment with Flashpoint 19 Kit. It uses 80W power that doesn't emit too much heat, so you could even have it closer to you, especially if you plan on doing close-up shots.

I would like to make one last recommendation if you need something lightweight that can be mounted on the camera. It's the iKan iLED-MA Micro Flood Light, which costs about $29.99. It can emit a dimmable wide 120-degree beam of bright 5000K+ Daylight with 21 1.2-watt LEDs. It comes with a MicroUSB cable for charging and a shoe mount fixed to a back holder so you can position it vertically or horizontally once it's on your camera.

The Tripod Or Stabilizer

You can opt for a tripod or a gimbal stabilizer, depending on how you shoot your videos. They both accomplish the vital task of keeping your image steady, which increases production quality. Most beginners opt for a tripod, so I'd recommend you start there too. Most of them are under $100 on Amazon, and they work well, especially if your camera is light enough. If you need something sturdy and more durable, a few options will keep the bank, including the iKan E-Image EG01A2, for only $169. This tripod can handle most DSLRs and camcorders and holds up to 11lbs. The extension of this tripod is over 5 feet, making it easy to shoot from exciting vantage points. The best part is that it can collapse to 33 inches and weighs only 10lbs, making it ideal for travel.

I recommend the iKan FLY X3-Plus Gimbal Stabilizer gimbal stabilizer, which goes for $69.99 and is perfect for content creators continually shooting on the move. Let's face it: no matter how steady your hands are, handheld shooting will produce shaky and jarring videos. This gimbal is fantastic because it has a 3-axis stabilizer system with brushless motors to smoothen your camera movements. It also has a battery life that can last up to 5 hours! Talk about good value.

Video editing software

Post-production is just as important when aiming for high-quality video, so you must invest in some editing software. If you have a Mac computer, of course, you've got the free iMovie that comes with it (Windows Movie Maker for PC users). Still, you may want to consider other products in the market.

There's software that comes highly recommended by many of my peers, and it has a free version that a beginner can use to test out. It's called Hitfilm Express. It has professional-grade VFX tools. They claim it's perfect for beginners, gamers, or any creative who needs a budget. It might be worth checking out.

Adobe Premiere Elements 18 is an alternative many videographers promote. Of course, you need a budget for this and some skills, so give yourself time to learn how to use it best. If you'd like something easier to work with, I recommend Camtasia, which will cost about $199. It's easy to navigate and versatile. The learning curve is short, so if you're not too crazy about graphics and editing, that should sort you out. Need more software options? Keep reading this book as I cover more alternatives in an upcoming chapter.

For those who want to get fancy, add the following equipment.

Digital Recorder

If this is your first time hearing the term "digital recorder," don't worry. You're not alone. We've all had to learn what it is and why we need it. Usually, only the pros get this type of fancy equipment because they want to elevate that sound quality. At first, I hesitated to invest in it, but after using it for a few years, I can't believe it took me so long to get it. A digital recorder is helpful because it transforms any environment into a studio-like effect. This will be a worthwhile investment if you like crisp, high-quality sound. I especially recommend it if you'll be doing many interviews. A great one to start with is a Zoom H4N pro. It's handy, easy to carry around, and lasts a while.

Teleprompter

Another fancy piece of equipment you could get is a teleprompter to help you flow better with your script. It will ensure your message is on point and save you hours of filming and editing. Nowadays, various varieties can work with a camera or a smartphone. Amazon should have plenty of options, but you can always check out Caddie Buddy, which is pocket-friendly and functional.

Get a studio backdrop.

The last fancy piece of equipment you can get is a studio background. If you plan an indoor setup with minimum movement, consider getting a green screen or whatever studio backdrop fits your budget. Some of these can be quite costly, ranging thousands of dollars, so research first. When I'm shooting, I just opt for a natural background in my home with a bookcase in the set showing some of the awards I've received over the years. Nothing fancy. For my personality and audience, it works. But suppose you want to go for something flashy. In that case, you can check out this inexpensive backdrop I found on Amazon for $58 called Slow Dolphin Fabric Video Studio Backdrop Kit.

One recommendation I can make here is to create a large banner with your branding. Depending on the size, it could be anything from $100-$500, but when designed well, it can be a great way to reinforce your brand and make you look super professional.

Best Practices for Recording Your Videos

• **Make sure your video has a purpose.**

Don't just shoot a video because you heard the topic is trendy or because you promised your audience to post daily/weekly. Each piece of content should be planned on time. It should also serve a purpose. So, ask yourself, "What does this video want to accomplish? Is it views back to my website? New subscribers? More comments, likes, and shares? I encourage you to get laser-focused on one specific target.

• **Make the video valuable and relevant.**

Your video needs to add some value to your audience and potential subscribers. Whether you're a comedian, gamer, vlogger, stylist, personal trainer, or coach, ensure the content is relevant and valuable. If you're an entertainer, entertain and leave the viewer renewed and amused.

• **Do what it takes to have great audio.**

You might need more money to invest in expensive equipment, but you can still produce good-quality audio. If people can't hear you well, it doesn't matter how many filters and post-production software you use.

• Always have a teaser at the beginning of the video.

Any video content you create should always have a tease at the beginning, promising a specific result if someone watches the video all the way through.

• Have a call-to-action at the end of each video.

Many YouTubers shy away from this because they are afraid of seeming pushy, but the only way people will turn into fans, customers, and subscribers is if you ask them to act. Always ask them to do something if they received value at the end of the video and enjoyed watching your content. It can be as simple as subscribing or leaving a comment for you. You can also ask the viewer to like, share, or DM. Or you take it a step further and can ask them to head to your website to download something for free.

• Lighting is crucial if you want people to view more of your videos.

If people can't see or hear you clearly, you won't retain their attention for long. So, having the right light is equally important as investing in good sound quality. I shared lots of alternatives for lighting equipment earlier. Even if you can't invest in any, you can still create something that looks good if you stand in front of a large window. As you can see, the more natural sunlight falls on your face, the better the image quality.

#1 Tip for All Beginners

The best advice I could give you is to shoot one video daily. It's the first tip for all beginners who want to thrive on YouTube. If you ask any seasoned content creator, they will insist that you train yourself to create at least one piece of content daily. Why? There are several reasons.

The first thing this will do is raise your confidence and ability to shoot great videos. The more you practice using your equipment experimenting with different angles, lighting, sound, and content topics, the easier it becomes and the more natural you appear on camera. The second reason you want to shoot a video each day is to enable you to re-watch yourself and quickly pick up the mistakes you tend to make. Check your body language and posture. Notice how well you get into the flow and tempo of your script.

One last reason is that shooting videos daily ensures you have lots of content available, increasing your posting frequency. The more you can create a consistent publishing schedule whereby potential subscribers realize they can receive fresh, relevant content from you daily, twice, or three times a week, the more likely they are to subscribe and keep checking your channel for the latest stuff. It will build that connection and sense of community with your audience quickly. With all that said, consider challenging yourself to attempt to create a video each day for the next 30 days. There are many "Video Challenges" and contests on social media groups today that you can join.

Even without joining a group challenge, if you are serious about becoming a YouTube superstar, you can commit to yourself, block out time on your calendar over the next 30 days, and begin.

Shooting Techniques for Beginners

Whether you use a smartphone, camcorder, or a DLSR camera to shoot your videos, here are some tips that will give you that professional look even if you're a total amateur.

Tip #1: Always shoot landscape.

By landscape, I mean horizontally instead of vertically. That is especially important to remember when using your smartphone.

Tip #2: Use the overlay grid if you have it on your device and observe the Rule of thirds.

The Rule of thirds is something all pro videographers know. It's about placing your head slightly higher than the frame to give yourself visual breathing and walking space when facing the sides. Using a grid will guide you and help you position yourself correctly to maintain eye level with your audience. Otherwise, you will come across as looking awkward. The viewers will struggle to maintain eye contact as they watch you.

Tip# 3: Create stability for your camera.

You can invest in a tripod, or if doing a home video, you could get creative and stack books to help your camera remain still.

The more still your image, the better the quality will be. Avoid shaky filming unless you want to come across as a complete amateur and give your viewers a nauseating feeling. Investing in stabilizers and a good tripod is necessary if you're doing an outdoor recording with many movements.

This creative bonus tip will make you look like a pro. If you're shooting at home or in a home office, get a flat surface like a table and stack it with books. Place your laptop on top of the stack, and if you're shooting from your smartphone, place the phone on the computer for extra support and stability. You'll be amazed by how good the shot will be.

Tip #4: Time your shots.

I've seen several pro videographers sharing these hacks, and ever since I started implementing them, my videos have improved significantly. You time your shots by ensuring no sudden movement or change of scenery for about 10 seconds between each shot. That means you need to record with that in mind. You can have a different scene every five to ten seconds but only go as long to retain the viewer's attention. Remember, your videos will look way more professional when creating your outline or storyboard.

Tip #5: Keep a simple background.

It might be tempting to be fancy and outlandish with your background, but simple tends to produce a better quality-looking video. If you're shooting from home, remove as much clutter as possible. I also recommend shooting in front of a plain white background. Please avoid doors or windows where people could unexpectedly pop up and ruin the shot. If any elements appear in your camera, ensure they add to your story and do not distract viewers from your content.

Tip#6: Be intentional with your lighting.

This must be one of the biggest secrets for getting that professional look and feel. If you have a budget, invest in the different types of lights you'll need to achieve your desired look. If you're on a budget and can only work with natural sunlight and a few lamps, then get creative. Experiment with different angles and light setups to make your equipment work for your space.

Tip #7: Experiment with different angles.

I want you to create extra creative shots to produce exciting video content when shooting different scenes. It also ensures you have some backup or safety content in case you need to edit out some parts of the video. As much as possible, get some shots above and below your main recording vantage point. You don't need to have several cameras. Hit pause, move to a different angle, and hit record following the script or outline.

Tip #8: Keep the editing in mind during filming.

You need to know where you will make cuts, add filters, change scenes, etc. If you have this in mind while shooting, it will make the filming and editing process faster.

Set And Follow a Realistic Schedule

One thing you should know is most of the time; you're going to be completely off with your timing. I cannot emphasize the importance of setting the right expectations for yourself and creating a schedule you will stick to. Many YouTubers fail and give up because they could have done a better job creating a plan they could stick to. Most of them underestimated how long it would take to go through all the different shooting phases. Unfortunately, that led to stagnation, procrastination, and eventually defeat.

To help you avoid falling into that trap, we need to give you direction and a strict schedule that you must commit to. I can only offer guidance when it comes to creating your plan.

It would be best if you customized it to suit your needs. Depending on your lifestyle, whether you're currently working on other projects or a job, raising a family, etc., your schedule will match your case. If you're working full-time and need to start this after working hours, your shooting schedule recording space and editing need to be that. Maybe you can shoot daily after work, then edit and prepare them for publishing over the weekends. If you're flexible enough to shoot during the day and edit in the evenings, build your schedule around that. Regardless of your choice, understand that you must set a definite time for scripting, recording, editing, and publishing the content.

Pre-production tips:

Make sure you block out time for research, scripting, and even storyboarding if you're going in that direction. Plan out the different shots and scenes that you wish to have. I'd recommend making a shot list and ensuring you have the location or setup space needed for the photos and the necessary gear.

How long will a single shoot take? That will vary from person to person. If you have experience being on camera and know how to use your equipment, you can do it quickly. But often, it takes much longer than any of us anticipate. So whatever estimate you give yourself, permit at least 60 - 90 minutes longer.

To help minimize the time it takes, I encourage you to keep time limits on yourself. For example, set a five-minute timer to do all the technical setup. Also, give each scene a time limit and allow yourself to reshoot a scene twice before moving on to the following prominent location. That way, you won't have to recreate the whole thing.

Post-production tips:

So far, we've focused most of the content on shooting. We need to address post-production as well. Review your script, storyboard, or outline, depending on your work. This is important to ensure you filmed everything. Start the editing process. If you're editing yourself, you need software like iMovie, Camtasia, or another solution. You need to upload the different pieces of your video to the software and organize them in their proper order so you can decide what to keep and what to discard.

If you have enough coverage, picking and choosing the perfect ones would be easier, making this process faster. If you only shot once and there were many mistakes, give yourself time and patience. Such cases will require much refinement to get the video ready for publication.

What elements can you add to the video? You can use photos, b-rolls, interviews, titles, sound effects, transitions, intro and outro, music, and your logo.

Create thumbnails.

Use Canva or your preferred graphics creator software to create a compelling thumbnail for your video. Make sure it's attention-grabbing and helps the viewer know what the video will be about. In an upcoming chapter, we'll discuss how to create epic thumbnails.

Watch your video at least once before publishing. Make sure you watch the video at least once with a friend or family member to get some feedback. If you want something else, manage it to keep the flow and quality intact.

Once you feel it's ready, export it and upload it to YouTube. Depending on your experience level, this entire post-production process could take an hour, a few hours, or several days. When just starting, allow yourself a full day of post-production for each video if you want good quality. With lots of practice, that duration will significantly decrease.

If you decide to batch post-production, shoot videos daily, edit them on the weekend, and ensure you have enough videos ready for the upcoming week.

Implementation Activity #7: You Have to Do It

It's time for you to act and record your first videos. Your challenge in this section is to commit to a thirty-day video challenge. Keep yourself accountable and choose the setup and equipment most accessible to you. Every day, you will shoot a ten-minute video that's valuable and relevant to the viewer.

You can choose to post-produce one by one or batch them up. But make sure the recording happens daily. By the end of thirty days, you should have thirty videos of ten minutes each. Please make sure they are of high quality technically and that they deliver in terms of content value.

CHAPTER 08

Editing Videos

Video editing is an integral part of creating awesome YouTube videos. It can be as simple as removing unwanted footage, creating a flow, or as complex as adding effects, graphics, music, and giving a video a particular angle. Depending on your editing goals, you can spend a few minutes to several days or weeks. I always suggest setting simple goals and striving for progress instead of perfection for beginners. If you want your videos to look like a Marvel production in the first few months of editing, then be ready to invest a ton of time.

My best advice is to understand the basics and allow yourself to grow with your skills as you continue to shoot more videos. In this chapter, I will teach you the main elements, share the tools I recommend, and walk you through adding music to your videos. Let's get started.

Understanding the Basic Elements of Video Editing

Before sharing the main elements you need to consider when editing, let's clarify some jargon you'll often hear during this process.

• Crop Factor

The crop factor is a number that represents the ratio of a sensor's imaging area to that of a full-frame sensor. It's usually 1.3-20.

• Aspect Ratio

The relation between the width and height of your video is the Aspect ratio. The most common are 4:3 (This is the standard-definition video), 16:9(standard high-definition video), and 1.85:1(used for most U.S. theatrical showings since the 1960s). If there's one thing you'll need to remember, it's 16:9, as you'll use that one the most.

• Close Up

You'll often hear this term: shots that frame the subject tightly. For example, a close-up would fill the entire screen with your face if you were shooting in front of the camera.

•B-roll

This is additional footage meant to either smooth out an incongruent scene or provide more details for the story. Suppose you're talking about cooking ingredients and want to shift into a new location where you start demonstrating. You could add a still image of the elements you'll use to create a seamless transition from your talking head to you standing behind the kitchen counter, ready to cook.

- **Jump Cut.**

These cuts should only be used if you want to come across as an amateur. They are abrupt changes between sequential clips and often make the subject too jumpy from one scene to the next, disruptive for the viewer.

- **J-Cut**

Not to be confused with the other term; this is when you place the audio from the next shot before the video.

- **Resolution**

Resolution is the actual number of horizontal and vertical pixels your video contains. The most common are SD 640x480, HD 1280x720 & HD 1920x1080.

- **Shot List**

This is a checklist of all the shots you want to include in the production. Shot lists help you avoid wasting time and money and ensure you plan.

- **The Rule of Thirds**

The Rule of Thirds is a helpful grid used when shooting to make your video production aesthetically pleasing. To do it properly, separate the screen into nine sections. The Rule of Thirds suggests that points of interest line up with the intersections on the grid.

- Tilts are vertical movements made with your camera that are fixed.
- Pans are fixed horizontal movements made with your camera. Think of them as the opposite of tilts.

You are getting the pacing of the story right. Every video has a certain pace and tempo to it. Some scenes might need to be slowed down; others might need to speed up, etc. When creating your video, make some breathing room for your viewers to digest the essential parts of your video. That might include changing the speed in certain sections but ensuring a smooth and gradual transition to avoid confusing the viewer.

• Adding the proper transitions and special effects

We already mentioned this earlier. Adding special effects during editing, such as titles, transitions, and text effects, is a great way to make your videos look professional, but only if you know what you're doing. If in doubt, don't add fancy effects. The more natural your video is (without too many abrupt transitions and confusing impact), the better it will look.

• Choosing the right sound and music

That can include sound effects, audio background music, or anything else you think will make the video more impactful. Music usually adds a great atmosphere and increases that emotional connection, especially when done right. However, ensure the piece is non-intrusive and doesn't repel the viewer or obscure critical audio cues.

Understanding the technical and subjective things that cause people and YouTube algorithms to perceive your video as sound quality is essential.

A good video communicates a specific message. If it's an educational, inspirational, motivational, informational, or entertaining video, the viewer will come out on the other side having received that particular benefit. Therefore, a good video must add lots of value.

• **High quality**

Producing a high-quality video is as simple as following all the instructions outlined in this book. They include no shaky imagery, proper lighting and sound, avoiding noisy backgrounds, working on the script or outline, etc.

• **Clean and professional-looking editing**

This is another vital thing to remember when going through your post-production process. Keep things clean and simple. Only choose the best footage and eliminate what doesn't need to be there. Use elements like filters, music, sound effects, and transitions tastefully. Let everything on that video help you tell the story and pass on an easy-to-understand message.

• Ideal length of content.

A good quality video isn't too long and tedious or too short and unhelpful. You must pick your ideal length and ensure it's as long as necessary to accomplish the video's purpose. We talked about giving each video a specific purpose to fulfill. Let that be the guiding star when determining your videos' length.

• Attention-grabbing thumbnail and intro

Most people will never click on a video if the thumbnail isn't enticing. Do you know that about 20% of people who click on your video will exit after the first ten to fifteen seconds if you could better retain their attention? Even worse, these people are likelier to give your video a thumbs down within that first fifteen-second period. Therefore, you must ensure a strong intro and graphics that draw people in.

Once someone sees your awesome thumbnail and clicks to view it, you need a killer intro that immediately teases why they should watch to the end. Set expectations right and make them feel personalized. That builds a connection that ultimately creates trust and that sense of "this guy/girl knows what they're doing."

• Branded intro and outro footage

Add an intro and outro footage that aligns with your brand. This branded content gives new and existing viewers an impression of who you are and why they should continue hanging out on your channel. It makes you memorable, especially if you do it right. Given how many videos are uploaded each minute of the hour, and most viewers watch hundreds of videos across different channels, adding this branded content to your video will make it pop. It will increase the viewer's chances of recalling your brand the next time they come across your range on YouTube or elsewhere on the Internet.

Video Editing Tools That Every YouTuber Must Know

Now, let's talk more about editing tools that can help simplify post-production.

- **Adobe Premier Elements**

Adobe Premier has been an industry leader for a long time. It does cost a significant amount to get the software going for about $79.99. Now, there was a time when it was the ultimate; however, with recent advancements, many new players offer the same or even better at a fraction of their price.

It is still an excellent option for beginners and has many guided tutorials to make the learning curve swift. Its simple interface and suggested edits will get you going in no time.

- **Adobe Premier Pro**

As the name suggests, this software goes pro and offers you some of the best functionality you can find today. One of its best features is the Lumetri Color tool, which features color adjustment and manipulation close to what you'd get in Photoshop. It also has a multi-cam feature, allowing you to work with unlimited camera angles. The interface is easy to use, even for a beginner, and comes with a monthly fee of under $20.

- **Apple iMovie for Mac users.**

Suppose you are a Mac user and wish to refrain from investing in third-party software. In that case, you can create cool-looking videos with Apple's free editing software, which offers various transitions, sound effects, etc. You can easily do a montage, standard cut, J-cut, wipes, and almost every other editing effect. It's free and easy to use once you get the hang of it.

- **Apple Final Cut Pro X**

If you love iMovie and feel ready to go all the way, this software might be the one for you. This software comes with all the bells and whistles and can even superimpose 3D titles over your videos. It has a hefty price tag and could be a more straightforward interface. Still, you want to be a serious contender and produce incredible professional videos. In that case, you can transition from iMovie to Final Cut Pro for a one-time payment of $ 299.

- **Filmora from Wondershare**

Filmora is Wondershare's standard, high-quality, and easy-to-use video editing software. You can upgrade to unlock more sophisticated features. Still, I suggest starting with this one because the design is intuitive. It has filters, overlays, motion elements, transitions, and much more - basically, everything you need as a beginner. I love Filmora because all it takes is an easy drag and drop. Thanks to their easy mode feature, you can choose themes, select free royalty music, and end up with a fun, polished video. And compared to some of the prices I just shared, this one is pretty good because it starts at $59.99 for a lifetime license or $39.99 for a year.

- **Pinnacle Studio 21**

Pinnacle Studio 21 is another excellent and easy-to-use software with a drag-and-drop feature. It's intuitive, has a short learning curve, and has effects like 360-degree and stop-motion, making it stand out. It has top-of-the-line rendering speed and goes for a one-time payment of $129.95.

- **Lumen5**

While Lumen5 is more of an editing tool than software, I am still adding it here because of its increased popularity. It's great for creating fun, shareable videos and can even turn your blog content into video. So, if you have an existing blog, this is an excellent option. You can create as many videos as you want with their free version for 480p videos. If you're going to edit in 1080p HD, you must invest $50 monthly.

Adding Music to Your Videos

Background music can elevate your video and help build a

stronger connection with your audience, but you can't just throw in any song. You need to become aware of copyright restrictions and opt for royalty-free music. You should also choose a theme that supports the unfolding story or message of the video. You're wondering where to find great music.

YouTube offers some music options, and some software comes in-built with sound effects and free royalty music, but I recommend you research online. Go to sites like Epidemic Sound or Royalty-free Music to find stock music you can use.

Adding music to a video using Mac:

Once in the iMovie interface, you should see the Audio tab under the main menu bar within your new project. A drop-down menu will appear, allowing you to go into iTunes, Sound Effects, or GarageBand. In most cases, you must select iTunes and see a list of all your files. Then, it would be best if you dragged it down to the project timeline. If you need to trim the song, use the handles at the beginning and end.

Adding music to a video using Windows:

Double-click a video file to open it, and you'll see it opens in Movies & TV. Instead of that option, right-click the file and select Open With > Photos. You'll see a toolbar; click Edit & Create, then select Create a video with text. You'll then see Photos's editor screen and a Music button should be in the top toolbar. Click that and set your Music. After choosing the file, drag your selected clip down to the storyboard at the bottom of the screen. And when you play, you should hear music in the background.

Adding music online: Visit addaudiotovideo.com, and you can add music to your video without downloading any software. It's fast and straightforward. Once on the site, click Browse under "Select video file" to choose the video. Next, you want to choose the audio file by clicking Browse. Once you've selected both audio and video, click on Upload and give it a few minutes. Once it's ready, you'll see a " Completed " message and a download link.

YouTube Music: If you'd like to use YouTube's Audio library once you upload the video, click on the Editor and look for the audio row. You'll see a list of tracks you can listen to, and once you find what you like, add it to your video. If you'd like to adjust which part of the audio is played during your clip, click the Position Audio button and drag the song's leading and trailing edges to change their position.

Activity #8: Start Honing Your Skill

The videos you've started creating from the last chapter now experience your art. Your assignment is to begin implementing all the editing techniques, hacks, and guidance you've received in this chapter.

Remember, this is a skill that takes time and practice. As with all things, it will get easier. I suggest you allocate time specifically for editing your videos, whether you do one at a time or batch a few of them together. You can opt for free software or invest in one of the many examples I've shared throughout this book.

Your assignment is to open your editing software, upload your first YouTube video, and start editing. See if you can add a few transitions, a title, and background music to create an attractive flow with your video. Don't get too fancy. Please keep it simple. Once it's ready, please give it to a trusted friend or family member to watch for some helpful feedback.

SECTION 04

Managing Your YouTube Channel

YouTube channel management goes beyond uploading videos. Optimization, involvement, analysis, and adaptation continue. We discuss the complexities of channel management and offer tips for simplifying your plan, increasing audience engagement, and assuring long-term success.

YouTube Channel Success Tips

Sound management may help your channel succeed. Make appealing titles, descriptions, and tags that match the content. Write descriptively, using terminology naturally. Tags will classify your movie, so choose wisely.

An intriguing thumbnail may boost click-through rates significantly. It must look good and convey the video's message. High-quality videos should always be uploaded. YouTube supports several file kinds, but the most significant user experience is with high-quality videos.

Videos in relevant playlists help visitors browse and stay longer on your channel. Comments let you connect with readers and establish a community. Answer questions, acknowledge remarks, and lead group conversations to keep the mood light.

YouTube's analytic tools can help you evaluate your channel. Look at demographics to know your audience. Increase core audience engagement by making content more relevant. Watch time and retention measure viewer involvement. Information with low retention may need to be changed or made more intriguing.

Knowing where your traffic comes from—organic searches, suggestions, or other sites—can help you improve your marketing. Likes, shares, comments, and subscriptions indicate involvement. These show popularity and affect YouTube's recommendation systems.

YouTube SEO increases platform visibility like website SEO. Find relevant keywords for your essay and organically incorporate them. To improve SEO, include keywords in the first few lines of your video's description.

Making your content accessible with subtitles/closed captions provides more indexable content. Join the Discussion Now! YouTube rewards discussion-generating videos. Discussions on videos, especially immediately after upload, may improve their popularity.

Nobody views your YouTube channel alone. Off-site

interactions may grow your community and viewership. Share your films on Twitter, Instagram, and Facebook. Create social media-specific content to promote your products.

Collaboration with other YouTubers may generate something extraordinary. This may expose your channel to more people. Join niche forums, groups, and communities off-platform. Join arguments and provide helpful content.

YouTube and the internet are constantly evolving. Follow YouTube's algorithm, feature, and policy developments. Trends: Following current events and viral challenges can inspire material and increase reach. Regularly solicit viewer feedback. It engages listeners and offers advice.

YouTube channel management is constantly evolving. You must understand the platform, know your audience, and be flexible enough to adapt to market changes. The proper channel management approaches focus on building a loyal, engaged audience around your content rather than chasing views. Even as you grow, sincerity is crucial. Your voice will distinguish you in YouTube's vast globe.

CHAPTER 09

Best Practices for Managing Your YouTube Channel

One thing about YouTube you need to remember is that it's both a search engine and a social networking platform. So, while it's essential to implement everything you've learned so far, I also want you to be deliberate with certain aspects of search engine optimization, as that will enable your videos to perform well longer.

Brian Dean of Backlinko is a specialist in search engine optimization, and you can learn a lot by subscribing to his YouTube channel. But let's touch on the key things I've learned from the best SEO guys in the marketplace.

Creating Video Titles, Descriptions, And Tags

Assuming you have a comprehensive list of the keywords you wish to rank for in any video, the title, description, and tags are where you need to sprinkle those pre-determined keywords strategically.

YouTube Video Title has a limit of 100 characters, so you need to use this space to build curiosity, create an emotional response for the viewer, and still add your keyword. Aim to place the main keyword at the start of the title as much as possible or at least within the first 70 characters so that it's viewable in the search results.

YouTube Video Description has a limit of 5,000 characters, so you've got plenty of space here to communicate your message and add relevant keywords. The first three lines are the only visible part of the description, so I recommend having your primary keyword here. You must also describe and sell the viewer into watching the video here. Remember to include the relevant URL you'd like people to visit after watching your video.

Throughout the description area, I'd aim to sprinkle the primary keyword about three times and other secondary ones to support your SEO.

YouTube Video Tags can be up to 30 characters, and you can add up to 500 characters in the tag section. Add the primary keyword, any words that describe the video's content, brand-related or channel-specific tags, and any LSI (Latent Semantic Indexing) keywords you might have.

YouTube Thumbnails

It would be best to have thumbnails that attract the viewer to get potential subscribers to click on your videos. Thumbnails are also the first thing searchers will encounter on Google and YouTube search results. The first thing you need to know is the ideal size. Google recommends 1280 by 720 Pixels with a minimum width of 640 Pixels and an aspect ratio of 16:9. It should also be formatted as a JPG, PNG, or GIF for the best results. Make sure the file size is at most 2MB for easy upload.

Remember to use attention-grabbing texts, fonts, colors, and images when creating your thumbnails, but do what is necessary. Ensure the thumbnail is relevant to the content people will find once they click and that it's congruent with your brand identity.

If you're working with a graphics designer, they'll take care of these technical aspects, but if you're going solo, I suggest using Canva. They are free graphics design software that requires little to no experience and even have pre-made templates. You can also purchase their royalty-free images for $1, and they offer a pro version that unlocks even more features. Another tool that can help you create awesome thumbnails is Spark by Adobe. Check out these online tools to find the one that suits your objective.

Uploading Videos

Uploading videos to YouTube is as easy as signing into YouTube Studio and clicking Create > Upload Video. Once you've selected the video you've finished editing and processing, YouTube will take over and do its thing until it is ready for publishing. The video file format recommended is MOV,

MPEG4, MP4, AVI, WMV, MPEG-PS, FLV, 3GPP, WebM, DNxHR, ProRes, CineForm, or HEVC (h265)

If you want to upload a video longer than 15 minutes, you must go through a quick verification process where they will send you a security code through your cellphone. Once your channel is verified, you can upload up to 12 hours or 128GB.

You can upload up to 15 videos at a time using your computer. And don't worry if you accidentally close the upload page. The video is usually saved in drafts until you finish choosing the settings.

If you want to upload high-dynamic range (HDR) videos, you can do it directly to the platform. Viewers can watch HDR videos with compatible devices or stream HDR videos using Chromecast Ultra to an HDR TV. If the viewers don't have a compatible device, they will see the video as a standard dynamic range (SDR). Although HDR videos can't be edited with YouTube Web editor once the video is uploaded, YouTube will automatically convert HDR video to SDR.

Once the video renders and completes processing, you can add basic info, including an SEO-friendly title, description, and tags, and upload your thumbnail. You can also choose more advanced settings and how you want to monetize if you're eligible. We'll be talking more about monetization options in the last section. If you're happy with the settings and preview of your video, it's time to share it with the world.

Creating A Trailer Video

The trailer or welcome video can be one of your most fun activities. It doesn't need to be an expensive production. But it will require lots of creativity and time investment. I've seen some epic trailers (check out the Slow Mo Guys Channel Trailer to see what I mean). You can start from scratch or get a template from online platforms like Biteable to simplify the process.

The actual process of a welcome video is super easy. Like any other video content, you must create, edit, upload, and hit publish on your channel. The only difference is that you want to head to the "Customize Channel" section with a trailer video and upload the video from there. Once uploaded, you can add SEO-friendly data like tags, descriptions, etc. The last thing you will need to do is set the video as the YouTube channel trailer by clicking "For new Visitors." That way, anyone who lands on your channel for the first time will always see that video.

Some best practices for the trailer video:

Keep the video brief and concise (under 30 seconds is ideal). Think of it like those epic movie trailers, and share all the necessary information about your channel. Your viewers should feel like they understand what you're all about and how they'll benefit by subscribing, but it should still leave them hungry to learn more.

The best trailers have a great story, implement their brand identity through the music, fonts, colors, etc., and always incorporate a call to action.

Categorizing Your Videos into Playlists

YouTube playlists are similar or related videos on a particular subject. You can create a playlist using your videos or curate other people's videos to get people to binge-watch and stay on your channel. It will help with the discoverability of your rut and increase watch time, which, as we know, will help rank your videos higher on search.

Go to Video Manager > Playlist to create a playlist, then select New Playlist. Give your playlist a name and click Create. You can also create playlists as you navigate YouTube. This is especially important if you're curating videos. When you find a video you'd like to curate, click the plus icon to add it to an existing playlist or create a new one. You can make your playlist public, unlisted, or private, depending on your preferences. It's also possible to optimize your playlist for search by editing the title and description with a specific keyword and a compelling explanation telling people why they should watch.

Pro Tip:

If you want your playlists to stand out, consider adding an intro welcoming the viewer and offering tips or letting the audience know what they can expect by going through each video on the playlist. This can work exceptionally well if you're creating an educational video series.

Creating YouTube Stories

If you're a fan of watching YouTube from your smartphone, you already know about YouTube Stories. Previously known as YouTube Reels, these are like Instagram or Snapchat Stories. They can only be viewed on the mobile App. Viewers access them either from the channels or Watch pages of their subscriptions.

YouTube stories aim to increase that bond and connection with your community. It needs to be done in a very informal and casual way. You need to make sure it's a regular activity so people can get used to interacting with you directly.

You can add an image or video to a YouTube Story. To add a photo, tap the capture button like when taking a regular print. Suppose you want to record a video; press and hold the capture button until you're done recording. Stories videos can only be 15 seconds long, so make sure it's short and sweet. Plenty of editing tools are available to add elements that will help make your content more appealing. You can also edit aspects of your recording and even delete an existing video or image from your story. Tap the story and play segments to navigate to the video or photo. Look for the three-dot menu and tap Delete.

Applying SEO

Now, let's talk about ranking factors and how to apply SEO to your videos. Throughout this book, we've discussed the importance of using keywords strategically. As I shared earlier, Google says ranking factors are important—relevancy, interest, etc. You will agree with me; there must be more that we can do to stand out.

Given that over five hundred hours of video are uploaded each minute, we need many more tools and techniques to ensure our videos get promoted by the algorithm. Here are a handful to add to your toolbox. You already know the basics, i.e., Keywords, title optimization, description, tags, and producing high-quality video, so let's talk about new ones.

• **Watch Time**

Watch time is a huge ranking factor for YouTube. It's the time a viewer spends on your video before clicking away. The longer a session, the more the algorithm will favor your content.

• **User Experience and Engagement Level**

That includes how much people comment, like, dislike, share, and subscribe after watching your content. Videos with higher engagement will be ranked higher.

• **View Count**

Getting many views on your video matters. Putting more pictures equals a higher ranking, especially if you've optimized your keyword.

• Closed Captions & Subtitles

Adding closed captions to your videos benefits you in multiple ways. The main two are: 1) you get crawled by search engines faster, which can give you a significant SEO boost, and 2) you open your content to a broader audience. People who are not natives of your spoken language can easily understand you, increasing the chances of more engagement and subscription to your channel.

Mastering The Use of YouTube Analytics

Your channel will only grow successfully by combining front-end creative efforts with back-end tracking and monitoring. YouTube has an in-built analytics system to track the right metrics and build your dream business. To get started, you must sign in to your creator studio and find your way to the main menu's analytics Tab. You'll see the last 28 days by default, but you can customize it to suit your needs.

If you enjoy data crunching, YouTube allows you to export datasets as Excel or CSV. However, most of us let the system do the manual work. All we need to monitor and track, especially at the beginning, are:

- Watch time reports
- Interaction reports
- Revenue reports

With watch time, you want to answer questions such as, how long are people watching my videos, and how many views do I have in the chosen timeframe? Is it the same as last month? Who is watching my videos? Where are my viewers located? What are some sources of my traffic? What percentage of my views come from mobile, desktop, or elsewhere?

Interaction reports will show you things like subscribers, likes, dislikes, comments, and sharing. You can see how many new people subscribed and how many unsubscribed. You can see how your audience feels about your content and whether they resonate with your message. Monitoring comments is also important because it gives you a sense of how active and engaged people are. Remember to be responsive but don't get sucked into the world of troll hunting or toxic people.

When it comes to revenue reports, this is all about the monetization of your money. You've been waiting to hear about it because your money will be recorded here. The following section will discuss monetization and how to do it right. For now, recognize that this is where you will come to monitor your revenue within a given period, including your paid ads on YouTube, Ads other companies are paying to display on your videos, and other income streams like YouTube Super Chat. The main thing to track here is the estimated income from all Google-sold ads and the projected revenue from AdSense and DoubleClick ads.

Promoting Your Channel on Other Social Platforms

It's essential to think outside the box to grow your channel. It would be best if you were discovered, and your channel needs to escape obscurity. Everything this book outlines will enable you to set the proper foundation for that, but you must continue. Social platforms like Facebook, Instagram, TikTok, and LinkedIn have so much traffic. With some creativity, you can get more views on your video. How? By driving that traffic toward your YouTube channel. You don't need to get in front of YouTuber users only. You can also leverage organic and paid strategies to promote your channel on other social platforms.

For example, you can write articles on high-traffic sites like LinkedIn or Medium and embed a video or link back to your YouTube for free. But of course, you could take it further with a little paid ads budget. Do this by creating an epic video ad for Facebook or Instagram that drives traffic back to your YouTube channel for the whole experience. Once you look at your YouTube analytics and determine the location and audience type that best engages with your track, invest a little money and run a highly targeted ad on Facebook to bring in more of the same people. Please refer to the resource section to learn more and expand your traffic source strategies.

Continuously Learning from Others

As you can tell, this book is only the beginning. Something easy to follow to help you gain some momentum. The journey is long, and there's much to learn, so make sure you continue educating yourself as the platform evolves and new hacks emerge. One way to stay up to date and discover the best and latest hacks is by following and initiating friendships with fellow YouTube creators. You can join meetups either locally or virtually. You can also attend events like VidCon or Social Media Marketing World. I have included links in the resource section to learn more about these opportunities.

Activity #9: Start Tinkering Around

This chapter shared lots of technical knowledge that will only work if you apply it to daily activities. If you have not worked on previous exercises, now is the time to do that. Once you have that video ready to share with the world, make sure also to include the things you've learned in this chapter, including:

- Creating your thumbnail.
- Uploading your video to YouTube.
- Customizing and optimizing the video titles, descriptions, tags, and any other effects you wish to have, such as music, captions, and subtitles.
- Follow a YouTube creator from whom you want to learn more as you grow your channel.

CHAPTER 10

Growing Your Community

YouTube is all about community engagement. If you're unwilling to spend time and effort building a connection with your tribe, you won't do well on this platform. Having read this far, I'm confident you want to grow a channel that serves your tribe and makes you money. To hit both targets, we need to understand some strategies that will enable us to draw in more eyeballs.

Sources Of Traffic

Do you know how your video can be discovered on YouTube? I've mentioned several throughout this book, but it's worth listing them here.

- YouTube search
- YouTube advertising
- External websites
- Browse Features

- Suggested videos
- A particular playlist or channel page.

You need to figure this out as your channel grows so you can refine your SEO efforts and invest in the right strategies.

Using The Audience Tab

Did you know YouTube Analytics offers an inside glance into your audience's behavior, location, and preferences? This tab shows you where most of your viewers are located, the language they speak, what they love watching most, and their age group. You need to be signed in to your YouTube Studio to see this. From the left menu, select Analytics > Audience. That will open information on gender, age, when your viewers are on YouTube, and other videos your audience watched. Use this data to inform your content strategy.

Engaging Your Audience

As a YouTuber creator, your job is only done once you interact and engage with your audience. A few things that work well for engaging my audience include initiating engagement myself. That means I don't just post and wait for something to happen. Instead, I go and find content that's meaningful to me, and I like, comment, and share that content. I also reply to every comment and intend to do that until it becomes too much for me to handle.

I've set aside twenty minutes weekly to visit the channels of people who have liked or engaged with my content. I do the same on their channel, which creates impressive rewards later. Consider asking questions that benefit your community and encourage them to interact. The bottom line is you need to give more than you ask of your community. If you observe highly engaged channels from YouTubers like Gary Vaynerchuck or Neil Patel, you'll see they always give, give, and give before making any ask.

Pro Tip:

If you're serious about showing your community that you care, take a screenshot of a comment left on your video or a video title shared by someone you want to promote. Create a video out of that featuring their content. It will cause the person to respond immediately and even share your video.

YouTube Community Tab

This is a feature YouTube designed to promote community interaction. It's meant to help you interact even more with your people beyond creating and publishing videos. You will have the ability to post polls, text-based posts, and images.

This feature is meant to give your channel a different edge and to get even more personal. You can also promote older videos or products and merchandise. However, ensure you balance the promotion and the value-adding interactions. It is an incredible way to excite people about something you're doing. It could be the launch of a new product, an announcement of a free webinar, or training.

I have used the Poll feature to get ideas of what to include in my online course to make it more valuable. My friend Jeremy uses it to give behind-the-scene sneak peek of his latest documentary shoots, which excites people. The most important thing is to come from a place of adding value. Give people a reason to interact and follow your updates using the Community Tab feature.

Maximize The Use of Live Streaming

What is Live Streaming? It's being able to record and broadcast in real-time simultaneously. YouTube has become famous for live streams, and it is the perfect way to retain or draw in a new audience. You will need to educate yourself on the best equipment for live streaming, but YouTube enables you to go live from your smartphone or tablet, a camera, or a computer. Once you get the kit sorted, it takes one button click.

Before attempting to go live, verify your channel (www.youtube.com/verify). If doing it from a computer, you must sign into your dashboard and click Create > Go Live. Open the YouTube app from your mobile, click the camcorder icon on the top right, and then tap Go Live. If it's the first time to livestream, you must wait for 24 hours to activate your account. Also, note that you must hit your first milestone of 1,000 subscribers before live streaming from your mobile.

When it comes to the recording, you can either do it through a webcam, mobile cam, or encoder streaming. The easiest option is the camera on your laptop, but if you want a more professional look and have the competency, you can always get an encoder because the quality will be better.

To ensure you produce the best live streams, have your thumbnail image, an SEO-friendly title, and description ready. If you're ready to record from your desktop, click the camcorder icon once you're in your dashboard >Go Live > Webcam. Add a title and privacy settings, click More Options to add the description, turn live chat on/off, promote something, and more. Click Next. YouTube will automatically take a webcam thumbnail photo, but don't worry; you can upload the thumbnail we created later. Select Go Live, and that's it! Once you're done, you can select End Stream.

A Checklist for Optimization

Here's the beauty of live streaming - it's live. There are no do-overs or edits. So before you begin to broadcast, take the following steps.

• Check the audio to ensure the sound is optimal and that people can hear you.

- Adjust your lighting to ensure the audience can see you.
- Keep the devices plugged into a power source. You wouldn't want to run out of power halfway into your rant!

- Test your connection speed to avoid low-quality streaming. You can run a speed test with speedtest.net. What we are aiming for is about 10MB of data per minute.
- Turn off interruptions and ensure nothing inappropriate or confidential is in the backdrop.
- Have a bottle or glass of water next to you. I also recommend tissues or anything else you might need if you get a scratchy throat, cough, or sneeze.

When it comes to live streaming, timing is everything. There's no perfect time per se, but based on your YouTube analytics, you can make an educated guess based on your audience interactions and behavior. If most of your audience is global, you want to pick a time that works in multiple time zones.

Pro Tip:

As your audience grows, you can consider running polls for people to vote the best time for the live streaming, and once you have a winner, schedule it in advance. Give people time to add it to their agenda and set reminders.

Activity #10: What Moves You?

Before we hit the last section of this book, it's time to start engaging with your potential audience. You may not have any subscribers yet (aside from friends and family), but you can still create that momentum for engagement. If your published videos have received many comments, shares, and likes, you can find channels worth interacting with. Leave a comment, like, and share it. Repost it using your Community Tab, as you learned in this chapter. Demonstrate that you are here to build an active community. It all begins with you.

SECTION 05

Monetize Your YouTube Channel

YouTube exploration goes beyond video creation and management. The chance helps many artists generate money. Monetizing your YouTube channel may transform your pastime into a business. Here are several ways to generate cash from your track and be reimbursed.

YouTube Income: The Easy Way First, learn YouTube monetization basics to make money with your videos. The YouTube Partner Program (YPP) is its primary revenue source. You can apply for YPP with 1,000 subscribers and 4,000 watch hours in the last year. Advertising can start when your movies are approved.

YouTube has display advertising, non-skippable video commercials, skippable video ads, and bumper ads. Understand potential revenue sources by learning about them. You can limit ads to the film's beginning, middle, or end. Keep the watching experience enjoyable by finding a balance.

YouTube Income Without Ads. Besides standard ads, there are

other techniques to boost channel profits. Promote your items and affiliate links in your movies. Each referral link sale earns you a commission.

A firm pays you to market their products or services in sponsored content videos actively. To be honest with readers, label such content "sponsored." If you have a loyal fanbase, selling branded t-shirts, mugs, and posters is a good idea. Your channel's premium subscribers should receive a badge, emoji, or additional content. Viewers may pay to have their comments "pinned" to the top of the chat window in your live broadcasts using "Super Chats."

YouTube Moneymaking: YouTube's monetization rules maintain content quality and community standards. Video material must comply with YouTube's advertising restrictions. Content that's contentious or offensive may not sell.

Avoid unlicensed use of protected works. Copyright strikes may limit monetization. Be transparent about paid promotions and other relationships to maintain audience trust and platform compliance.

They are diversifying income sources. Online services like YouTube are dynamic, so don't put all your money in one basket. Creatives receive direct audience funding via Patreon. You might offer premium materials or other incentives as recompense.

Presenting paid seminars or lessons online may be an option if you have vast knowledge. Private consultations: Offer expert guidance and counsel.

Money Management and Investments. Financial management becomes more critical as your channel grows and income rises. Record all income and expenses regularly. Consider your income tax. To be safe, consult a tax specialist. You may invest income in the channel to improve it. New technologies, visuals, marketing tactics, or staff may be needed.

YouTube channel monetization is an art and science. Understanding the platform's technical needs is vital, but success comes from being authentic, consistent, and valuable to your audience. Monetization should increase content quality and trustworthiness. It would be best to prioritize trust and transparency with your followers as you negotiate the YouTube revenue market. YouTube channels are valuable for the relationships they build, not for their revenue.

CHAPTER 11

YouTube Monetization Made Easy

For many readers, these last two chapters contain the answers to critical questions that led them to purchase the book. If you have been wondering how to make money on YouTube or what kind of money you could make, this is where you'll get your answers. How much money do YouTubers make? Some make zero, while others make millions in annual revenue. The range is vast because it depends on how well the channel performs.

How Much Can One Earn on YouTube?

The best way to approach this question is to start from what we know YouTube pays out. We know that Google pays 68% of their AdSense revenue. Some quick mathematics will show that if an advertiser pays $100, Google will pay $68 to the publisher. An advertiser's rates will vary between $0.10 to $0.30 per view, but let's go with an average of $0.18 to make calculations easier. So, on average, your channel can receive $18 for every 1,000 ad views ($3-$5 per 1000 video views).

While these simple numbers can help you estimate what you can expect, realize the first dollar will be the hardest to earn. Building up to that momentum will require tremendous effort, but the more subscribers you have, the more people will click on your ads. The more that happens, the more money you will make from

Google AdSense and other opportunities. So the correct answer is - you can earn as much money as you want. It all depends on your effort and strategy. If you're in a niche that quickly gathers crowds, like celebrity gossip or gaming, you'll likely start earning money sooner, but still don't expect it to be within the first couple of videos. In the first phase of your YouTube growth, you want to focus on building a reputation instead of income. Then, as you get real traffic and engagement, you'll see the revenue growth from a few dollars each other to hundreds and, ultimately, thousands of dollars each month.

The Simplest Way to Earn Money From YouTube

The simplest way to earn money from YouTube is to join the YouTube Partner Program (YPP). You will need an audience before becoming part of this program and making money. Your content must be epic to attract an audience that engages with your content and subscribes to your channel. Everything discussed in this book is designed to help you attract, build, and monetize your audience. Once you have momentum and see constant growth, I recommend applying for the YouTube Partner Program.

To qualify for YPP, you must be in good standing with YouTube. Your content should be considered high quality. You also need 4,000 public watch hours within the last 12-month period. Lastly, you will need to hit that target of 1000 subscribers. These basic requirements are vital before your qualification can be accepted. Once you cross this threshold, you'll be taken through creating an AdSense account and a few other simple logistics. The YouTube team will review and approve you for monetization. Besides streaming ads, you can earn through channel membership and Super Chat as long as you meet their criteria.

Activity #11: Become A YouTube Partner

This activity will require time, so I recommend adding it to your planner or setting a timer so you can return to the designated time to complete it. Once the channel grows in the coming months, and you cross that threshold of 4,000 watch hours within 12 months and 1,000 subscribers, please submit your application for the YPP monetization opportunity.

CHAPTER 12

Creative Ways to Make Money on YouTube

Now that you've established a great YouTube channel that is steadily growing, it's time to focus on making money. Combining several revenue-generating strategies might be the right approach if you want to start seeing income from all your hard work. Instead of depending on earning directly from YouTube (YPP), which requires a specific number of subscribers and strict watch time regulations, you can leverage other moneymaking options such as affiliate marketing, sponsorships, etc. Let's go over the main ones now.

Become An Affiliate

Affiliate marketing is one of the easiest and most lucrative ways to earn an income on your channel. The best part is that you can use a small audience. In recent years, brands have sought micro-influencers and social media channels with decent-sized following and lots of engagement to help promote their products.

Franck is an excellent example of this. A software company approached him about a month ago and gave him a very enticing offer. Franck was provided the free software for six months and would earn a percentage for every person who signed up and purchased through the affiliate link they gave him. The best part is that Franck has 2400 subscribers! It's only been a few weeks, and he's reported that a portion of his audience has signed up for the free trial, and some have paid. Income is already coming in, and soon, he will be making a projected $7k in passive income.

Affiliate marketing is simple. You have a product you believe in and a link to send people. Whenever people buy, you get a small commission. Monthly sales can earn anything from a couple hundred to several thousand if it's a well-priced product. I know YouTubers who also run affiliate products from Amazon and ClickBank. These are massive affiliate platforms that anyone can join. But I suggest doing this once you have an active audience.

Become An Influencer

Influencer marketing is all the rage. Stay-at-home moms, artists, beauty specialists, and high school students have all turned their love for selfies into income-earning opportunities. What is an influencer, and can you become one on YouTube? An influencer is a person who can affect the purchasing decisions of others because they are perceived as an authority in that given niche. Influencers have strong relationships with their audience, making them powerful. An influencer is not a celebrity and doesn't need to be a Kardashian with millions of followers. The size of their following depends on their niche or topic. Brands are always keen to work with influencers of all sizes.

If you can build a reputation as someone knowledgeable and an expert in your topic through your YouTube content, you can become an influencer. As a result, you can get paid partnerships, collaborations, and sponsorships with the brands that align with your channel. There are various types of influencers, including mega-influencers (think Kardashians). These are often celebrities like movie stars, musicians, athletes, etc. To join this rank, you must have at least 1 million followers. Macro-influencers are a step down from the mega-influencers. These are usually up-and-coming B-grade celebrities or super successful self-made online experts. You'll need at least 40,000 followers on YouTube to join this rank. Micro-influencers are the first significant milestone I would set for you. This category of influencers are ordinary people who have gained respect and recognition for their knowledge.

You can create a relationship with your subscribers; over time, they will see you as someone worth following and turning to for advice. In this category, it's not about the number of followers. It's absolutely about the relationship and engagement level. So a micro-influencer can have between 1000 – and 40,000 followers on YouTube. Franck is an excellent example of how a brand perceived him as a micro-influencer and offered him the chance to collaborate through affiliate marketing. The same thing can happen to you. As an influencer, the most important thing to remember is to maintain your integrity and promote brands you genuinely believe in.

Once you are an influencer, companies will offer you deals and opportunities to make money because they need your audience. Be intentional about the ones you say yes to because your audience is more valuable than any money a company offers. Always think long-term and think about what's best for your audience.

What kind of income can you make from influencer partnerships?

Depending on the size of your audience and the budget of the company or business you work with, you can earn a few hundred bucks to shoot one video or thousands of dollars to run a specific campaign over an agreed-upon timeframe. Influencer marketing requires planning, strategy, and a solid business plan to get paid what you're worth.

Sell Products and Merchandise of Your Brand

Another fantastic way to earn money as a YouTuber content creator is to create your merchandise. These can be T-shirts with your brand, coffee mugs, calendars, art, paintings, comics, recipes, or whatever else you can create for your niche. The best part about this is that you get to keep 100% of the profit. Use platforms like Shopify and Amazon to set up shop quickly, then leverage your growing audience to drive traffic to your online store.

Crowdfund Your YouTube Project

If you're not looking to support your YouTube career with ads, affiliate marketing, and selling merch, you could go the crowdfunding route. Some have found it highly successful. Unlike ads, you are giving your audience more of what they want. The focus here is content and engagement. Check out a channel like Hasfit, which mainly grew and still focuses on crowdfunding. You can crowdfund your channel through websites like Patreon or use the YouTube Sponsor Button, a newly established feature that lets your fans support your channel in exchange for some "perks" you give.

Fan Funding

As the word states, this is a way for your fans and subscribers to tip and support your hard work. The more great content you produce, the more likely you will build fans who love and appreciate all the effort and dedication you put in to serve them. If you want to create an easy way for people to "tip" you, then consider checking out a site like ko-fi.com, enabling you to receive tips or donations. You can also create a simple PayPal button that people can use to "buy you coffee" if they love your content and channel. Remember to make it easy for people to give you their cash by placing links under each video's description.

Social Media Marketing on YouTube

Social media marketing uses platforms to connect with an audience to market your products. If you get the right strategy, you can use social media marketing to grow your YouTube channel and sell products or services. The system can be both paid and organic marketing efforts, but I suggest using some paid social media advertising if you want to see results fast.

You can make money on YouTube using social media marketing by running ads on Instagram and Facebook that drive traffic back to your channel. You could also create a social media campaign offering a free lead magnet that leads to people sharing their data with you. Once you have that data, you can send people to your YouTube channel to promote whatever product or service you wish to sell, or they can be served ads through your YPP. If you'd like to learn more about social media marketing, a deep and vast topic, I suggest getting one of my other guides.

Applying YouTube to Your Existing Business

The benefits of integrating YouTube into your business marketing and development strategies are too numerous to mention. Let's start with the fact that your Search Engine Optimization efforts will exponentially pay off when you leverage video marketing. As the second-largest search engine on the Internet, having your videos rank high on Google will drive more traffic to your website. You will also develop an instant connection with your audience. Existing customers and prospects will feel more connected to your brand when you use videos to educate, inspire, and showcase your products.

We know content marketing is here to stay because today's consumer prefers to learn about a product, feature, or brand through sharable, informative content instead of traditional dry ads. By creating great videos, you're serving your potential customers' needs far better than your competitors, who might still be focused on conventional ads. Video marketing makes it easy for anyone with any budget to succeed because it's no longer about throwing money at ads to manipulate people into purchasing. People want to feel valued, and with video, you can show your audience that you care and that your product or service is the best solution. I cannot think of a better way to market to an existing or new audience than through video content and a great YouTube channel.

YouTube Advertising

YouTube ads are great for attracting customers or new subscribers to your channel if you have the budget. Introduce your brand or business using YouTube ads, and your track will grow exponentially. But it would be best to do more than throw money into this. Ensure you have a solid plan with clear objectives before spending a dime. YouTube isn't as inexpensive as Facebook and Instagram because it's a mature platform, so the learning curve necessary to pull off a great campaign is steep. Luckily, they have many resources, educational content, and even a certification process to empower you to use their powerful advertising features. You can go from knowing absolutely nothing about Google ads to setting up a successful ad campaign in no time with as little as $10 per day.

There are several options when it comes to ads. You can create skippable in-stream ads, non-skippable in-stream ads (including bumper ads), video discovery ads, and non-video ads (the overlays and banners).

To advertise on YouTube, you must upload a video and set it to Public or Unlisted. Then, sign into your Google Ads account and select New Campaign. Choose your goal (sales, website traffic, brand awareness, reach, or brand consideration. Please define your campaign parameters and budget, target your audience, and enter your link to hit the create campaign. And that's it! Your ad is live and ready to bring you a new audience.

Use storytelling and emotion to connect with your audience to get the most out of your campaigns. Have an appropriate call to action and consider using the correct type of ad for the specific goal. For example, if sales were your main objective, I recommend setting up a TrueView for an action campaign. That will allow multiple clickable elements so viewers can click and act before the video ends.

Sticking to the recommended length and video formats is also a good idea. Skippable ads should be a minimum of 12 seconds and a maximum of 3 minutes (you can have a max of 60 seconds on YouTube, kids). Non-skippable ads are 15 seconds (In Singapore, Mexico, India, Malaysia, and EMEA, they allow 20 seconds), and bumper ads are 6 seconds.

For discovery ads, YouTube recommends having AVI, ASF, QuickTime, Windows Media, MP4, or MPEG file format. The video codec should be H.264, MPEG-2, or MPEG-4. The audio codec should be AAC-LC or MP3. The aspect ratio should be 16:9 or 4:3; the frame rate most recommended is 30 FPS.

Activity #12: Optimization

You've made it to the last activity for this book. Here, it's all about optimization. So far, you've learned how to turn your growing channel into an income-generating machine. Take time to decide how to earn money and set up the necessary processes. If you're getting into influencer marketing, get a book and learn how to pitch, sell, and win deals with brands. You'll need to learn how to market yourself so that brands find you appealing.

Suppose you're getting into affiliate marketing or creating and selling your products; that will require some action steps to plot and implement. Use this time to figure out how to act on those activities that generate your money. You must also keep tweaking, iterating, and improving your channel's SEO. Monitor and track everything as you publish new content so your psychic can become a profitable YouTube business.

Conclusion

You have made it to the end of this book. We've given you lots of material and assignments to work with, so feel free. Each section of this book was placed in the order you must follow as a beginner.

The monetization section came last with good reason. A mistake many new YouTubers make is to focus on monetization too early in the game. As you put down this book, your main work is implementing the first three sections to the best of your ability. If you can get that done, monetization will be a natural by-product, and you will succeed.

You will only get very far if you develop the mindset, discipline, persistence, and consistency necessary for this journey. Again, let me remind you that your WHY must be more significant than your obstacles and the insecurities and doubts that will pop up along this journey. Your passion and desire to share your message, build a community, and serve others will determine how far you can go as a YouTuber.

The YouTube platform is one of the most powerful vehicles in 2021, where you can be, do, give, and share whatever you believe in. Done right, it will open opportunities and rewards beyond your wildest dreams. Many have started with an idea, built a brand over time, and turned a sad story into a YouTube empire. You have the potential to do the same. All you need is a plan. Each chapter of this book has given you guidelines and procedures, from setting up the channel to researching content, finding your brand's identity, and posting your first video.

You have learned hacks that will save you time and energy when editing and putting out professional-looking videos, even shooting from a basement. What you need now is a serious commitment to your dream. If you are ready to be a successful YouTuber, it's time to put in the effort and reap the benefits of having thousands or millions of people watching your content, taking your advice, and buying things from you. Whatever your end goal might be - a lifestyle of travel, sharing your passion with the world, becoming famous, earning a six-figure income, boosting your local business, or any other objective, the first step is to implement the lessons this book offers.

Resources

Ubersuggest's Free Keyword Tool, Generate More Suggestions. (2020, April 17). Retrieved October 21, 2020, from https://neilpatel.com/ubersuggest/

YouTube, Twitch, Twitter, & Instagram Statistics - SocialBlade.com. (n.d.). Retrieved from https://socialblade.com/

Southern, M. (2020, June 29). Google Explains How YouTube Search Works. Retrieved October 21, 2020, from https://www.searchenginejournal.com/google-explains-how-youtube-search-works/373189/

Filmmaker, D. (2019, November 10). Should I Start a YouTube Channel? We Asked These YouTube Creators for Their Advice. Retrieved October 21, 2020, from https://digitalfilmmaker.net/start-youtube-channel/

T. (2020e, May 25). 10 Most Popular and Profitable YouTube Niche Ideas. Retrieved October 21, 2020, from https://toughnickel.com/self-employment/10-Most-Profitable-YouTube-Niche-Ideas

Google Tool Find My Audience. (n.d.). Retrieved October 21, 2020, from https://www.thinkwithgoogle.com/feature/findmyaudience

Customize channel layout - YouTube Help. (n.d.). Retrieved

October 21, 2020, from https://support.google.com/youtube/answer/3219384?hl=en&visit_id=637391251673478626-2441383931&rd=1

Segev, L. (2020, August 26). The Importance of Branding for YouTube Creators: TubeTalk Episode 161. Retrieved October 21, 2020, from https://vidiq.com/blog/post/branding-for-youtube-creators-tubetalk-161/

Proud, D. (2020, February 13). Proud Business Productions - How To Customise Your YouTube Channel Layout. Retrieved October 21, 2020, from https://www.proudbusinessproductions.com/blog/2020/2/21/how-to-customise-your-youtube-channel-layout

Gardner, K. (2020, September 3). Quality is in the eye of the beholder: new research on what viewers love. Retrieved October 21, 2020, from https://www.thinkwithgoogle.com/marketing-strategies/video/video-production-quality/

Google. (2016, September). *Deep Neural Networks For YouTube Recommendations.* Paul Covington, Jay Adams, Emre Sargin. Retrieved from https://static.googleusercontent.com/media/research.google.com/en//pubs/archive/45530.pdf

Discover video traffic sources - YouTube Help. (n.d.). Retrieved October 21, 2020, from https://support.google.com/youtube/answer/9314355?hl=en

Vidcon Event. (n.d.). Retrieved October 21, 2020, from https://www.vidcon.com/

Thank You

You could have picked from hundreds of other books, but you bought mine, and I appreciate it. Thank you so much for purchasing my book.

Not that you enjoyed (I hope) my book, can I ask you for a tiny favor? Can you please post a review on the platform? You posting a review is the best way to support the work of independent authors like me.

Your feedback will help me keep writing the books that will help you get the desired results. It means a lot to me to hear from you.

I am happy for anyone to reach out to me for help, comments, collaboration ideas, or feedback at

brian@brianscottfitzgerald.com

Visit my author page with this link or Scan this QR code

https://www.amazon.com/author/brianscottfitzgerald.

Printed in Dunstable, United Kingdom

74105280R00104